Finding Peace in Times of Pain

By Pastor Robert L. Dickie

© Copyright 2020 Robert L. Dickie

All rights reserved. No part of this publication may be reproduced, stored in a retrieval system, or transmitted in any form or by any means—electronic, mechanical, photocopy, recording, or any other—except for brief quotations in printed reviews, without the express written permission from the author. Contact him at emmausroadpress.com.

ISBN: 978-1-7346822-6-7

By Robert L. Dickie

"The Lord is my light and my salvation;
Whom shall I fear?
The Lord is the strength of my life;
Of Whom shall I be afraid?"

—Psalm 27:1

By Robert L. Dickie

Table of Contents

Introduction	7
1. Christ Promises Peace In Spite Of Trials, Tragedies, and Troubling Times	13
2. How Does The Bible Teach Us To Handle Suffering?	27
3. God's Promise of Comfort For Groaning Believers	41
4. Samson's Riddle	53
5. "...So Great Salvation," Hebrews 2:3	69
6. Discovering The Peace Of Romans 8:28	85
7. How Shall we Sing The Lord's Song In A Strange Land?	95
8. Comfort Ye My People	113
9. Comfort For Those Who Are Discouraged	125
10. Comfort For Those Who Are Dying	141

11. Comfort For Those Who Are Lonely   161

12. The Peace Of God   173

Conclusion   185

Endnotes   193

By Robert L. Dickie

Introduction

When the apostle Paul wrote the magnificent words in Romans 8:28 "And we know that all things work together for good to them that love God, to them who are the called according to his purpose," he knew that the daily experience of believers was one filled with great sorrows and much suffering. As time and history have shown, some things never change. In the book of Job, we are told that "…man is born unto trouble, as the sparks fly upward." This proverb reminds us that just as sparks inexorably fly upward from the fire, so it is that all mankind has been born into a world filled with trouble and sorrow. We cannot change or escape this. Jesus also reminded His disciples, "…in the world ye shall have tribulation…" John 16:33. Suffering and sorrows are a fact of life. The Bible teaches us that we live in a fallen world. In this imperfect world we must learn to cope with bitter disappointments, terrible tragedies, heartrending circumstances, and many hard providences from God that we may never be able to understand this side of eternity.

As a pastor it has been my responsibility over the last forty years to seek, by the grace of God, to help Christians cope with the trials and tragedies of life. It has not been easy. There are many tears that seem impossible to wipe away from those with a broken heart. But I have found over the years that the Word of God is the best comfort to God's children who are going through times of sorrow and suffering. What did the Psalmist teach us in Psalm 66:12? Did he not tell us that the Lord God, our Creator, our Savior and Friend, would lead us through the "fire and water," which is symbolic of suffering and trials? Yet, on the other side, when we pass through the fire and the water we come out with a wealth of treasures. The Psalm reads, "...We went through fire and through water, but You brought us out to rich fulfillment." We grow best in grace when we pass through the storms of life. The experience that we gain and the spiritual growth is described as "rich fulfillment." Great saints are made through great sufferings. The true child of God never drowns in the flood of waters, nor does he die in the flames of the fires of trials. God brings us through them.

One of Satan's great schemes is to try to fill us with doubts concerning God's love for us. If Satan can cause us to doubt God's love, to somehow think that the Lord has forsaken us and does not care for us, he can cause us to suffer shipwreck of our faith. Let me remind you of how precious you are, dear believer, to the Lord. You are the "apple of His eye." "Keep me as the apple of Your eye..." Psalm 17:8. You are the object of His eternal love. "...Yes, I have loved you with an everlasting love; Therefore with lovingkindness I have drawn you." Jeremiah 31:3. You are His chosen treasure. "But you are a chosen generation, a royal priesthood, a holy nation, His own special people..." I Peter, 2:9. You are the silver and the gold that He has invested in and has only put you through the fire to refine you and to make you even more special. "...You have refined us as silver..." Psalm 66:10. Oh my dear friend, never forget how special you are to the Lord. Do you think that He who loved you so much that He gave His only Son to die for you would ever lose His love for you or forsake you? Never!

As I write this, we are currently facing some of the most difficult times that believers have ever had to cope with in the last hundred years. For example:

1. We are facing a deadly pandemic from the Corona Virus that threatens the entire world. Most of our nation is shut down and people are quarantined in their homes. This has been one of the greatest crises in the history of this nation.

2. We are facing an unprecedented economic crisis because of the Corona Virus that threatens our stability as a nation. People are losing their jobs, their homes, their savings and retirements. For the first time in our lifetime, because of the collapse of the housing market in the U.S. we see that an alarming number of people now owe more on their homes than those homes are worth. We are facing the real possibility of another depression much like the Great Depression of the twentieth century.

3. We are facing the threat of worldwide terrorism from Islamic extremists. This problem shows no signs of going away. Currently on the news is the very real possibility that the Taliban may topple the government in Pakistan and acquire nuclear weapons. For the first time in our lifetime it is a possibility that a terrorist group may be able to get their hands on a large number of nuclear weapons.

4. We are facing a cultural collapse that sees the death of Western Civilization as we know it. Indeed, many experts already have written the West off as having already died. The problems and perplexities caused by postmodernism and the death of Western Civilization is of grave concern.

5. We have seen the political discourse in this country sink to an all time low where there is hardly any civility left in the halls of public service. Many believe we are nearing a time of civil unrest. Never has this nation been so divided since the Civil War.

6. We are living in a time when the church of Jesus Christ has lost its vision, its power, and its relevance. We see the Christian faith languishing all over in the Western world. We lack great prophets who can thunder out with authority, "Thus saith the Lord!" We no longer have men like the men of Issachar who know the times and know what we ought to do. These are indeed difficult and troubling times.

What I hope to do in these brief pages is to share with you some of the many lessons that I have learned over the years from my own personal times of sorrow and suffering and also from the Word of God. The Christian is one who should, of all people, be able to face the sorrows and sufferings of life with great faith, hope, and courage. The believer knows who is on the throne, and he knows that the future is in the hands of an all-wise providence, who is orchestrating all events from the throne room of heaven. So yes, these are times of great concern, but they are also times in which we can trust the true and living God.

The contents of this book are a collection of some of my sermons at Berean Baptist Church in Grand Blanc, Michigan. These pages are taken from my sermon notes and were not transcribed as the actual sermon was delivered at the time. The main thing I wanted to accomplish here was to capture the main points and essence of these messages.

I pray that this little book will be of great help and comfort to all who read it. May our Lord and Savior Jesus Christ, who is too wise to err and too loving to be unkind, comfort you and sustain you in these difficult and troubling times.

And may we never forget that in our desire to find peace and comfort in the troubling times of life, we will find God's peace and His sustaining comfort most when we are serving and seeking to comfort others.

> "Do you often feel like parched ground, unable to produce anything worthwhile? I do. When I am in need of refreshment, it isn't easy to think of the needs of others. But I have found that if, instead of praying for my own comfort and satisfaction, I ask the Lord to enable me to give to others, an amazing thing often happens—I find my own needs wonderfully met. Refreshment comes in ways I would never have thought of, both for others, and then, incidentally, for myself."
>
> —Elizabeth Elliot

1
Christ Promises Peace In Spite Of Trials, Tragedies, And Troubling Times

"These things I have spoken to you, that in Me you might have peace. In the world you will have tribulation; but be of good cheer, I have overcome the world." John 16:33.

*T*hese were the words of our Lord on the eve of His crucifixion. The Bible never promises the child of God a life free from pain, suffering, sorrow, or death. These are experiences that every Christian must face and cope with in life. Not until we get to heaven will these experiences be removed from the human race.

Jesus Promised Peace In Spite Of Pain

Jesus spoke to His disciples and told them that even though they would have tribulations in the world they would also have peace. "These things I have spoken to you, that in Me you might have peace." John 16:33. The Apostle Paul tells us how to find peace in those crushing, devastating, and painful moments of life. In Philippians 4:6-7 he says, "Be anxious for nothing, but in everything by prayer and supplication, with thanksgiving, let your requests be made known to God. And the peace of God, which passes all understanding, will guard your hearts and minds thorough Christ Jesus." Notice we are to turn to the Lord in prayer during these difficult times. We lift up our prayers and supplications to the Lord. We do this with praise and thanksgiving. The Lord is then pleased to pour out upon His children a heavenly peace that passes all human understanding. There is no reason for a child of God to suffer through life filled with worry, fear, and anxiety. How could this be that such a peace can be ours in moments of suffering and sorrow? Jesus knew that peace does not depend on our outward circumstances but on our inward spirit and response to those circumstances. The teaching that Jesus had been giving His disciples in John chapters 13-16 was designed to prepare them for the sufferings and tribulations of life that were to come. Notice carefully that Jesus tells them that they will face trying times with a certainty. There are no exceptions. All of God's children will be tested by the tribulations of life. We live in a fallen world that is under a curse. This explains the presence of sorrow and suffering in our world. When you face these times of trial and suffering, do not conclude that this is unusual or that you are being singled out to be punished or tried. This is the experience of every Christian as they walk with the Lord. However, these times of sorrow will also lead us to rich seasons of blessing and peace.

The Result Of The Sin Of Adam And Eve

The Scriptures make it clear that when Adam and Eve sinned in the Garden of Eden, as a consequence of their disobedience, a curse came upon mankind. God said to Adam in Genesis 2:17, "But of the tree of the knowledge of good and evil, thou shalt not eat of it: for in the day that thou eatest thereof thou shalt surely die." This was not just physical death but also spiritual death. As a matter of fact, all of the sorrow, suffering, trials, and tragedies that man faces today are a result of the fall of man in the Garden of Eden. After Adam and Eve sinned and ate the forbidden fruit, God came to them and stated the tragic consequences of their action:

"Unto the woman he said, I will greatly multiply thy sorrow and thy conception; in sorrow thou shalt bring forth children; and thy desire shall be to thy husband, and he shall rule over thee. And unto Adam he said, Because thou hast hearkened unto the voice of thy wife, and have eaten of the tree, of which I commanded thee, saying, Thou shalt not eat of it: cursed is the ground for thy sake; in sorrow shalt thou eat of it all the days of thy life; Thorns also and thistles shall it bring forth to thee; and thou shalt eat the herb of the field; In the sweat of thy face shalt thou eat bread, till thou return unto the ground; for out of it wast thou taken: for dust thou art, and unto dust shalt thou return." Genesis 3:16-19.

Everything that man faces in the world today as far as sorrow and suffering are concerned have come to us as a result of the fall. In the book of Revelation 21:4 we read that after Jesus returns from Heaven at the end of time, He will remove the curse of the fall. Here is what Christ will do in that day when He returns: "And God shall wipe away all tears from their eyes; and there shall be no more death, neither sorrow, nor crying, neither shall there be any more pain: for the former things are passed away." Oh what a blessed day that will be when the curse is finally removed and the child of God will no longer be tormented and troubled by the sorrows and tragedies of life.

Living In A World Under A Curse

In the meantime, however, the Christian lives in a world that is under a curse. We do face times of trial and tragedy. We all have our moments of pain, disappointment, sorrow, and suffering. These are the facts of life. We can do everything in our power to make life as sweet and as tolerable as we can, but we will never be able to remove all of these experiences from the lives of our loved ones. Not until eternity will these hurts and pains be finally removed.

Paul the apostle opened his second letter to the Corinthians with this word:

> "Blessed be God, even the Father of our Lord Jesus Christ, the Father of mercies, and the God of all comfort; Who comforteth us in all our tribulation, that we may be able to comfort them which are in any trouble, by the comfort wherewith we ourselves are comforted of God." II Corinthians 1:3-4.

Why would Paul write these words if the possibility of all of God's people to face such times was not a real and imminent threat? God allows us to suffer in a fallen world, but He also gives us comfort and teaches us through these trials to praise Him and to give Him glory for the lessons we learn from them. Trials and sufferings are part of the School of the Spirit. Great saints and great Christians are forged on the anvil of suffering and sorrow.

Today, we are facing a number of very alarming concerns: a financial crisis; international terrorism; the threat of war; the possibility of famines; the spread of new and dangerous diseases such as the swine flu, also known as h1n1 virus; and worldwide unrest and calamity. Add to these things the normal experiences that people often face in life such as sickness; disease; death; tragedies from accidents; and the heartaches from loneliness, bereavement, aging, loss of memory, loss of friends and family, and a multitude of other human experiences. All of these things make life a fragile, difficult, and painful journey.

We instinctively ask ourselves why does sickness, death, sorrow, and suffering so often come to the child of God? There is no other answer besides the fact that we live in a fallen world that is imperfect because of that fall. However, Bishop J.C. Ryle, an English minister once made an interesting comment that might help us with this question:

> "The only explanation that satisfies me is that which the Bible gives. Something has come into the world which has dethroned man from his original position, and stripped him of his original privileges. Something has come in, which, like a handful of gravel thrown into the midst of machinery, has marred the perfect order of God's creation. And

what is that something? I answer, in one word, it is sin. 'Sin entered into the world, and death by sin' Romans 5:12. Sin is the original cause of all the sickness, and disease, and pain, and suffering, which prevail on the earth. They are all part of that curse which came into the world when Adam and eve ate the forbidden fruit and fell. There would have been no sickness if there had been no fall. There would have been no sickness if there had been no sin."[1]

Elizabeth Elliot, in her wonderful book, *On Asking God Why*, relates how a friend of hers was passing through a very difficult time with cancer and she learned from that experience to understand and appreciate what others were going through when they were ill. Elliot writes:

"A letter from a friend of many years describes her cancer surgery and its aftermath—an incision that has to be scraped and cleaned daily for weeks. 'It was so painful that Diana, Jim, Monica, and I prayed while she cleaned it, three times and some days four times. Monica would wipe my tears. Yes, Jesus stands right there as the pain takes my breath away and my toes curl to keep from crying out loud. But I haven't asked, 'Why me, Lord?' It is only now that I can pray for cancer patients and know how the flesh hurts and how relief, even for a moment, is blessed.'"[2]

In this case Elizabeth Elliot's friend learned to understand what others faced and endured by her own personal experience with cancer. The afflictions of life are good teachers that enable us to be able to sympathize with others and to minister to them in their time of need.

Be Careful What Advice You Give To Those Who Suffer

It is in these times of sorrow and suffering that many of us as Christians face, we receive the kind of well intentioned advice that Job's three questionable friends gave him. Job's three friends were more of a hindrance than a help. Job's three friends, Eliphaz, Bildad, and Zophar made many nasty and cutting remarks through the rounds of their discussion with Job. They smeared his character, questioned his faith, mocked his knowledge, and judged his relationship with God. They proved to be very unprofitable friends to this suffering servant of God. When Job's friends arrived, the best thing that they did for Job was to sit with him for seven days and say nothing. It was when they opened their mouths that they did great damage to God's servant by their mean and judgmental words. Eliphaz begins and strongly implies that Job suffered because of his great sin. This is a judgmental and pharisaical approach to Job. Bildad spoke next: "If your children have sinned against him, he has delivered them into the hand of their transgression." Job 8:4. Bildad is basically consigning Job's children to hell. This sharp and cruel statement had to pierce deeply into Job's heart. Zophar spoke next and continued in this same line of criticism. Job's response was predictable. Job cried out, "How long will you torment me and break me in pieces with words?" Job 19:2. We must be very cautious when giving counsel to those who are going through a time of suffering.

The advice of some people is meant to help, but many times can be more of a distraction than a real help. As a pastor, I have seen that when a member of the church is taken ill, there will be a rush to judgment, to speculation, to giving advice, that many times for the one who is newly diagnosed with an affliction only serves to confuse and to exasperate the situation. I feel that it would be better if most people would perhaps keep their thoughts to themselves or share them with the pastor and let him decide whether or not it would be in the best interest of the one who is sick to share these thoughts and ideas. Unless one is very close to the one who is sick, it might be better to leave giving advice to the minister and close family friends. For although your intentions may be well placed, it still can create a great deal of tension and unnecessary grief and distractions. Again, let me quote what Elizabeth Elliot shares from her own experience with the very thing I am speaking about. When she had loved ones passing through times of trouble, her counselors and advisers (well meaning as they were) multiplied. Questions and suggestions such as the following are given:

> "Is the primary condition enough faith for our part? We must scour our own hearts to see that there is no stoppage there—of sin or of unbelief. We must stand on the promise. We must claim such and such. We must resist the devil and his weapons of doubt. And we leap at and pursue any and all reports and records of healings. 'Look at what happened to so-and-so!' 'Listen to this!' 'I've just read this wonderful pamphlet.' We know the Gospel accounts by heart. We agree that this work of healing did not cease with the apostolic age. We greet gladly the tales of healing that pour in from all quarters in the Church—no longer only from those groups that have traditionally 'specialized' in healing, but from the big, old, classic bodies in Christendom—Rome, Anglicanism, Lutheranism, Presbyterianism, and so forth. 'God is doing something in our day,' we hear, and we grasp at it eagerly."[3]

We have all heard of the kinds of things that Elizabeth Elliot has spoken about here. Well-meaning friends and advisors rush to the sides of those who are sick and inundate them with all sorts of advice (whether they want it or not) that many times only confuses them and creates more hurts. I recall the time when a loved one died of cancer, and a letter was sent from a faith-healing ministry that laid the blame for the person's death on the doorstep of the surviving members of the family because, as the letter stated, "They did not know how to fight off the demons and the power of the devil." Such advice is not only cruel but is absolutely sinful. When we examine the Scriptures, we remember that not everyone was always healed or delivered from their illnesses or problems. Peter was delivered from prison in answer to the prayers of the church, but John the Baptist died in prison as a martyr. The widow of Nain had her son brought back to life, while many other mothers didn't. The apostles healed many, but there were times when others were not healed. Even the apostle Paul had prayed for a healing for his thorn in the flesh but did not have it removed. The will of God is sovereign in these matters. There are no cut-and-dried answers to the problems of suffering and sorrow in this world.

The Presence Of Trials, Tragedies, And Suffering

The point we must remember here is that Jesus has told us that we live in a fallen world. This world is under a curse. We can all expect that during the span of our lifetime we will all face our share of sorrows and griefs. "…in the world you will have tribulation…." In Greek, the word "tribulation" is *thlipsis*. This is a word that describes distress, affliction, or trouble that is very intense. Jesus is telling us that He had overcome all of these. If Jesus overcame them, we can as well.

We must not be surprised by the tribulations that we will face in life. We must be prepared to face them courageously and take our sorrows to the Lord to seek His help and comfort. It is a great mistake to conclude that the Christian life will be free from suffering. Jesus made it clear that this was not the case. The hymn writer understands this and says:

God Hath Not Promised

God hath not promised skies always blue,
Flower-strewn pathways all our lives through;
God hath not promised sun without rain,
Joy without sorrow, peace without pain.
God hath not promised we shall not know
Toil and temptation, trouble and woe;

He hath not told us we shall not bear
Many a burden, many a care.
God hath not promised smooth roads and wide,
Swift, easy travel, needing no guide;
Never a mountain rocky and steep,
Never a river turbid and deep.
But God hath promised strength for the day,
Rest for the labor, light for the way,
Grace for the trials, help from above,
Unfailing sympathy, undying love.
—Annie J. Flint

Jesus Gave The Proper Solution To Suffering

Jesus concluded our text in John 16:33, and said, "Be of Good cheer, I have overcome the world." Jesus overcame the world, He is continuing to overcome the world, and He will always over come the world. The answer to the trials and tribulations of life is to remember that Jesus overcame the world. "Be of good cheer" means to take heart, be encouraged, don't worry. His victory is our victory. We can overcome because He has overcome. When Jesus spoke this verse, He had not yet passed through the night at Gethsemane. He had not faced the two trials that were looming on the horizon. He had not yet been to the cross or risen from the dead.

But Jesus spoke with a certainty that though these things were soon to unfold, He considered them already accomplished. Nothing would or could prevent Him from accomplishing this great salvation.

The risen Savior who indwells His people has given His disciples the ability to be overcomers. Believers can overcome prejudice, hatred, discrimination, persecution, injustice, slander, insults, and injuries. We can overcome all situations through the power and grace that is ours through Jesus Christ. God's people have this amazing ability to forgive, to be forbearing, to turn the other cheek, to be humble in suffering, to even be willing to die as martyrs for the cause of Christ. As C.H. Spurgeon once said about life, "The way may be rough but it cannot be long."

2

How Does The Bible Teach Us To Handle Suffering?

"But recall the former days in which, after you were illuminated, you endured a great struggle with sufferings: partly while you were made a spectacle both by reproaches and tribulations, and partly while you became companions of those who were so treated; for you had compassion on me in my chains, and joyfully accepted the plundering of your goods, knowing that you have a better and an enduring possession for yourselves in heaven. Therefore do not cast away your confidence, which has great reward. For you have need of endurance, so that after you have done the will of God, you may receive the promise." Hebrews 10:32-36

From years of experience, I have found that when

counseling people who were passing through the fires of affliction that come from sickness, suffering, and sorrow, that the best comfort comes from the Word of God. It is especially helpful to be able to show to people who are suffering how the saints of God handled suffering in the Bible.

In the New Testament believers are exhorted over and over to be filled with joy and rejoicing. A study of the words *joy*, *joyful*, and *rejoicing*, will show that the general context of these passages is that believers are called upon to exhibit these attitudes in the presence of persecution and suffering. Hebrews 10:32-36 gives us a good starting point to see this point illustrated:

> "But recall the former days in which, after you were illuminated, you endured a great struggle with sufferings: partly while you were made a spectacle both by reproaches and tribulations, and partly while you became companions of those who were so treated; for you had compassion on me in my chains, and joyfully accepted the plundering of your goods, knowing that you have a better and an enduring possession for yourselves in heaven. Therefore do not cast away your confidence, which has great reward. For you have need of endurance, so that after you have done the will of God, you may receive the promise."

The Greek words here are certainly describing the sorrows and sufferings that the people of God often face in life. Commentator William R. Newell states:

> "These Hebrew believers, in their earlier experience—the former days after they were enlightened, had endured a great conflict of sufferings...had had compassion on them that were in bonds, and took joyfully the spoiling of their possessions. Here is constancy in suffering and trial. They had come to the Cross; they had believed on the Son of God, who had borne their sins there and had returned to Heaven in resurrection blessing. Their unbelieving countrymen treated them as they had treated Christ Himself. Look at the words, gazing-stock, reproaches, afflictions, bonds, spoiling of possessions! And how did they endure? In the knowledge that they had for themselves an abiding possession on high!"[1]

How New Testament Believers Handled Suffering

How did these New Testament believers who are mentioned in our text in Hebrews display such grace and patience during the trials and afflictions that they were passing through? This text gives us some clues. First, they responded joyfully to the spoiling of their goods and the plundering of their possessions by unbelievers during persecution because they believed that in heaven they had an inheritance that could not be taken away. Jesus told His disciples this very thing in Matthew 6:19-21:

> "Lay not up for yourselves treasures upon earth, where moth and rust doth corrupt, and where thieves break through and steal: But lay up for yourselves treasures in heaven, where neither moth nor rust doth corrupt, and where thieves do not break through nor steal: For where your treasure is, there will your heart be also."

Christians are people who live their lives with an entirely different perspective from the unsaved people around them. Christians live with their eyes on eternity. And no matter what happens to them, believers know that they have an inheritance in heaven that no one can plunder or steal from them.

Secondly, Christians were taught to be patient, that having done the will of God they would eventually receive the promise of future blessing and reward, "For ye have need of patience, that after ye have done the will of God, ye might receive the promise." (Hebrews 10:36).

In a similar fashion the Apostle James taught his readers to be joyful when times of trial and testing came upon them. James writes:

> "My brethren, count it all joy when ye fall into divers temptations; Knowing this, that the trying of your faith worketh patience. But let patience have her perfect work, that ye may be perfect and entire wanting nothing." James 1:2-4.

Commenting on this text, British author Gordon J. Keddie said:

> "Few statements can be more calculated to raise the eyebrows than this invitation to what looks like a species of masochism. It is one thing to believe that some disaster may be a so-called 'blessing in disguise'; it is quite another to regard it with joy! The standard heroic response to trials is to keep a 'stiff upper lip' or, in the USA, to invoke the spirit of the pioneers: 'When the going gets tough, the tough get going.' But 'pure joy'? This makes the mind boggle. It grabs our attention. It

is certainly not what we hear from the counselors and psychiatrists of our time."²

Christians know that God rules the universe. They know that God is also sovereign over the affairs of life; therefore, true Christians have come to learn that they can trust their heavenly Father. When trials and tribulations come, they have learned to rest in the loving providence of an all-wise God. They have been taught to conclude that every sorrow and every difficult situation has some eternal purpose to teach them and to prepare them for heaven or perhaps to prepare them for future service to the Lord here on earth. Have we learned what these believers mentioned in our text learned? Have we learned to turn all of our burdens over to the Lord? Peter tells his readers in I Peter 5:7, "Casting all your care upon Him, for He cares for you." The "cares" that Peter mentions in this text are the burdens, the worries, the problems, the painful situations that we face in our lives. It is one thing to remember that Jesus cares for us; it is another thing altogether to cast our burdens upon Him and let Him carry them and bear the load.

Many Christians, instead of casting their burdens on the Lord, will carry them; they will worry sick over them; they will groan under the weight of them. They are doing something that is so foolish. Why carry, worry over, or be crushed by the things Jesus has already taken care of? If you think that God is not big enough to carry your sorrows, then by all means stoop down in your foolish stupidity and see if you can carry the load. But I offer you a better way. Let the eternal God of the universe carry them for you as He promised He would. Dear brother and sister, look across the horizon. Do you see a vast number of weary pilgrims trudging along, stooped over by the weight of their burdens, as they struggle to carry the cares of the world on their shoulders? You say, "Yes, I can see them!" These are Christians who dishonor the Lord by concluding that He is not big enough, great enough, or kind enough to carry the "cares of life" as He said He would. There is no need to struggle with the weight of your cares and burdens unless you are very sure that the Lord is not able to carry them for you. I say that facetiously. You will never face a problem too big for God.

How Old Testament Believers Handled Suffering

When Joseph, the son of Jacob, was sold into slavery by his brothers, he learned not to be bitter but to see that this cruel providence was from the Lord. The story of Joseph is one of the most beautiful and powerful examples of "grace under fire" that we find in the entire Bible. The story is found in the book of Genesis. Joseph is sold into slavery and his brothers tell his father, Jacob, that a wild animal killed him. The brothers even take Joseph's coat that their father gave to Joseph and dipped it in the blood of an animal to convince their father that Joseph was indeed dead. Jacob believes the false report and lies about the supposed death of Joseph, all the while Joseph is taken down into Egypt to languish and suffer as a slave. The remarkable preservation and exaltation of Joseph in Egypt is absolutely astonishing. Joseph, through a series of amazing providences, is eventually exalted to the highest position in Egypt next to Pharaoh himself, all the while his father, Jacob, has grieved over his son and thought him to be dead. When a famine in the land of Canaan brings Joseph's brothers to Egypt to purchase grain, Joseph reveals his identity to them. His brothers are filled with fear and trembling and imagine that Joseph will take revenge upon them for the cruel deed of selling him into slavery. But Joseph, who suffered through all these years, had learned a powerful lesson from the Lord. One of the great verses in the Bible on how to handle suffering and disappointment is found in Genesis 50:20. In this verse Joseph addresses his brothers after their father, Jacob, had passed away. The brothers thought that now that their father was dead, Joseph might be tempted to exact some kind of revenge upon them. So Joseph's brothers sent a messenger to him to plead for mercy. Joseph's response is a timeless principle of grace, love, and mercy for all believers to learn. Joseph said to his brothers, "But as for you, ye thought evil against me; but God meant it unto good, to bring to pass, as it is this day, to save much people alive." Genesis 50:20. Over the centuries, many of God's people have resorted to this precious text to help them respond in kindness and grace to their enemies. This story enables us to see beyond present circumstances and helps us to understand that God is on the throne and has eternal plans for every painful moment of our lives.

What a promise we also have in Jeremiah 29:11, "For I know the thoughts that I think toward you, saith the Lord, thoughts of peace, and not of evil, to give you an expected end." The Bible reminds us that God has gracious and wonderful thoughts and plans for each of our lives as believers. God knows that we are His workmanship. We are clay in the hands of the Master, who molds and shapes our lives by His providences. We may not always understand what the Lord is doing by allowing our hurts and sorrows, but we have this confidence that the Lord knows better than we, and He will, perhaps, someday make it plain. The words of hymn writer Maxwell N. Cornelius, speak well to this point.

Not now, but in the coming years,
It may be in the better land,
We'll read the meaning of our tears,
And there, some time, we'll understand.
We'll catch the broken thread again,

And finish what we here began;
Heav'n will the mysteries explain,
And then, ah then, we'll understand.
We'll know why clouds instead of sun
Were over many a cherished plan;
Why song has ceased when scarce begun;
'Tis there, some time, we'll understand.
God knows the way, He holds the key,
He guides us with unerring hand;
Some time with tearless eyes we'll see;
Yes, there, up there, we'll understand.
—Maxwell N. Cornelius

David also teaches us in the Psalms how to handle adversity and afflictions. In Psalm 119:67 David says, "Before I was afflicted I went astray: but now have I kept thy word." The great Baptist preacher, C. H. Spurgeon, said of this verse:

> "Often our trials act as a thorn hedge to keep us in the good pasture, but our prosperity is a gap through which we go astray. If any of us remember a time in which we had no trouble, we also probably recollect that then grace was low, and temptation was strong...perhaps David would never have known and confessed his own strayings if he had not smarted under the rod. Let us join in his humble acknowledgments, for doubtless we have imitated him in his strayings…. Sweet are the

uses of adversity, and this is one of them; it puts a bridle upon transgression and furnishes a spur for holiness."[3]

The Psalms are full of comfort for those who are going through painful and troubling times. In Psalm 71:3 we read, "Be thou my strong habitation, whereunto I may continually resort: thou hast given commandment to save me; for thou art my rock and my fortress." I have seen over the years, not only from my own personal experience, but also from observing many of the Lord's servants, that one of the secrets of dealing with trials and tribulations is to find a refuge in the presence of God. Those individuals who know how to draw near to God and rely on God's grace are those who do so much better in these difficult times. The word *habitation* in our text is from the Hebrew word *maon* and means "a dwelling place, a residence or a place of safety." The Scriptures teach us that God is such a place for His people in times of trouble and testing. Psalm 91 uses this idea to encourage believers to draw near to God in the times of testing. Verse one of that chapter reads, "He that dwelleth in the secret place of the most High shall abide under the shadow of the Almighty." How do we make God our habitation and continually resort to Him? The answer is found in the idea of abiding in Christ. We need to develop the sense of the presence of God at all times. We, as believers, always live in the presence of God.

We are indwelled by His Spirit and we are never alone. In times of trial we must not forget this fact. We need to take steps everyday to be in the Word of God so that we can find strength and comfort from the Lord when we are passing through the fires of persecution or pain. Our God is a gracious God, who encourages, comforts, strengthens, and delivers His people from the tempests of life. I have tried to remind people that they need to develop a personal and intimate relationship with the Lord. He is our dwelling place; He is our habitation where we can run to find refuge, rest, and comfort in the storms of life. That kind of special relationship is only developed by a daily walk with the Lord. This happens when we draw near to God in prayer, in the Word of God, in fellowship with other believers, and in the means of grace by attending the worship services of our local church. Those believers who do these things will indeed find that the Lord is a refuge and a hiding place from the tempests of life. The benefits of drawing near to God and making Him our habitation is also seen in Psalm 40:1-3. David writes:

"I waited patiently for the Lord; and he inclined unto me, and heard my cry. He brought me up also out of an horrible pit, out of the miry clay, and set my feet upon a rock, and established my goings. And he hath put a new song in my mouth, even praise unto our God: many shall see it, and fear, and shall trust in the Lord.

This is a wonderful passage that shows us what the Lord is able to do to the one who makes God his habitation and who finds in the Lord that secret dwelling place from on high. There are five things that David tells us that the Lord may do for us when we run into His arms to find refuge and spiritual rest"

1. He comes to us.
2. He hears our prayers.
3. He brings us out of the horrible pit (our times of sorrow and suffering).
4. He establishes our life (goings).
5. And He puts a new song into our mouth, (He fills us with praise and joy in the midst of sorrow and suffering).

Psalm 46:1-3 is another text that shares something similar with us:

"God is our refuge and strength, a very present help in trouble. Therefore will not we fear, though the earth be removed, and though the mountains be carried into the midst of the sea; Though the waters thereof roar and be troubled, though the mountains shake with the swelling thereof."

This is a wonderful promise. Christians who have found themselves suffering and oppressed have been able to draw great peace and comfort from these words.

It is absolutely astonishing to consider the words of the Apostle in the book of Hebrews where he says that his readers had:

> "joyfully accepted the plundering of your goods, knowing that you have a better and an enduring possession for yourselves in heaven. Therefore do not cast away your confidence, which has great reward. For you have need of endurance, so that after you have done the will of God, you may receive the promise." Hebrews 10:34-36.

The Bible teaches us that there is a better way to respond to sufferings rather than becoming bitter, cynical, revengeful, and having a morbid "poor me" attitude. Only the grace of God can enable us to respond in this fashion. This is what makes the Christian so unique in this fallen and suffering world. Where others respond with hatred, revenge, and deep bitterness, the Christian is enabled to respond much like the Lord Jesus Christ.

By Robert L. Dickie

3
God's Promise Of Comfort For Groaning Believers

"And we know that all things work together for good to them that love God, to them who are the called according to his purpose." Romans 8:28

The Apostle Paul knew that the experience of the believer in this world often leaves us in a state or condition of groaning and sighing. He writes in Romans chapter eight:

"For we know that the whole Creation groans and labors with birth pangs together until now. Not only that, but we also who have the first fruits of the Spirit, even we ourselves groan within ourselves, eagerly waiting for the adoption, the redemption of our body." Romans 8:22-23.

We live in a fallen world that is under a curse. Suffering, death, sorrow, and the tragedies of life are often overwhelming. Indeed, we long for the coming of our Lord and the new creation with the new heaven and the new earth. But until the Lord returns, no one is immune from the sorrows and groans of life. We groan when we sin and long for deliverance from temptation; we groan when we are ill, or when we see others suffer; we groan when we read of wars and disasters; or hear of famines and starvation in far-away lands. Yes, life is very hard and is often filled with sighs and groans. Yes, this terrible groaning is our experience in life.

Now the Apostle comes to this great verse, which is among believers universally associated with comfort. The verse is Romans 8:28. This is one of the most amazing and mysterious verses in all of the Bible. It has been used by the Lord to bring comfort to all believers throughout the centuries. Every Christian has found himself, at one time or another, resting his broken heart on this sacred text. The Scripture reads:

> "And we know that all things work together for good to them that love God, to them who are the called according to his purpose."

I want to share with you God's promise of comfort for groaning believers. There are two things I want to accomplish in this message. First, I want to share with you the meaning of this promise in Romans 8:28. And second, I want to share with you how this promise works in our daily lives and every day experience.

The Meaning Of This Promise

So first, we come to the meaning of this promise. Paul begins with "And we know." He is writing to believers only. This pronoun "we" refers to Christians. He is not suggesting that all things work together for good for all people. He limits his comments to believers only. The question that arises is this: "How do we know that all things in life work out in the end for our good?" There are two ways that we have received this knowledge. First, because God tells us so in Scripture. This text, and in other places, the Lord has taught us this most important lesson. And second, our experience has also proven these things to be true. So both by special revelation and by personal experience we find that all things, good or bad, work together for good to those who love God. Next, Paul continues with, "that all things work together for good." What does Paul mean by, "all things." He means all things whether good or bad, joyful or sad, triumphs or trials. Note that Paul does not mean that "all things" are necessarily good. But he does mean that our wise, sovereign, and loving God is able to bring good, that is, something positive out of every hurtful or disappointing experience in life. God so orders all events and overrules all events that we can say everything works out for our good.

Paul next adds this clarifying statement: "To them that love God." Ultimately there are just two kinds of people in the world today: those who love God and those who do not love God. A more accurate translation of this text could read, "God works all things for good to the ones who are loving Him." Perhaps we should pause here and define what the apostle Paul means by loving God. Lovers of God are those people who:

- Keep His Son's commandments (John 14:15).
- Follow and worship His Son (John 10:27).
- Live for His Son's glory (I Corinthians 10:31).
- And those who walk with His Son (Genesis 5:24).

Finally, in our text, Paul says, "To them who are the called according to his purpose." This promise of Romans 8:28 is only true for those who are called by God. In the scriptures we see that there are two different kinds of "calls." There is a general call, which goes out to all men every time the gospel is preached, and then there is the effectual call, which is the call of the Spirit reaching into the hearts of all the elect. One verse in the Bible that distinguishes between these two calls is Matthew 22:14, "For many are called [general] but few are chosen [effectual]. We also see here a reference to God's purpose. There are people "called according to his purpose." In another place Paul spells this out more clearly to Timothy, his younger protégé or disciple:

> "Who hath saved us, and called us with an holy calling, not according to our works, but according to His own purpose and grace, which was given us in Christ Jesus before the world began." II Timothy 1:9.

God's grand purpose is to choose a people from out of the fallen masses of humanity and to give them as a gift to His Son to be His Son's holy bride. Again, it is the Apostle Paul who teaches this to us. In his letter to the church at Ephesus Paul said, "Just as He chose us in Him before the foundation of the world, that we should be holy and without blame before Him in love." Ephesians 1:4. And Jesus Himself taught us in John 6:37, "All that the Father gives Me will come to Me, and the one who comes to Me I will by no means cast out." Paul also taught the church at Ephesus, "Husbands, love your wives, just as Christ also loved the church and gave Himself for her." Ephesians 5:25. Finally, John tells us in the book of Revelation:

"Then I, John, saw the holy city, New Jerusalem, coming down out of heaven from God, prepared as a bride adorned for her husband.... Then one of the seven angels who had the seven bowls filled with the seven last plagues came to me and talked with me, saying 'Come, I will show you the bride, the Lamb's wife." Revelation 21:2, 9.

Because of this verse in Romans chapter eight, we can rest in the assurance that everything will work out for our good and for His ultimate glory. "And we know that all things work together for good to them that love God, to them who are the called according to His purpose." One Christian author, as a result of studying this text, exhorted his readers by saying to them, if this is true, then quit trembling and trust. Quit pouting and praise. Quit running and rest. Quit worrying and wait. Quit belittling and believe."[1]

How This Promise Works

Second, we want to examine and see how this marvelous promise works. We have explained the meaning of our text. We have defined our terms. We have examined each statement that is so rich and full of glorious truth. But now we must see if this great statement of Paul's is really true, or is just another hollow promise like so many others that come to us from the philosophers of the world. How does this promise work? Or, in other words, how does suffering, sorrow, sin, failure, tragedies, and the like work for good in the believer's life? In the midst of my groans, sighs, and tears is there really any good that comes out of all this?

Let me list seven ways that demonstrate how God brings "good" out of all "these things":

1. God will use these "things" to get our attention. Let me explain. All of us occasionally pass through times of spiritual dryness and aridity of soul where we see our love for Christ cooled. We may become spiritually tired and exhausted, and the Word of God seems to lose its effect on our lives. What shall we do at times like this? Superficial and shallow people simply inject another program into the church or create another busy activity to weary people who are already worn out and spiritually fatigued. God's method is to get our attention through these "things" that Paul is mentioning. A true child of God knows when God is calling for his attention. These "things" bring us back to our senses and help us to refocus and cause us to listen to the voice of God once more.

2. God will use these "things" to develop patience, godly character in our lives, and to mold us into the image of His Son Jesus Christ.

3. God will use these "things" to teach us how to pray, to trust, to walk with Him more faithfully. Dr. David Martyn Lloyd-Jones once said, "Christian people are generally at their best when in the furnace of affliction."

4. God may use these "things" to teach us humility. Struggling, suffering people are not self-assured, self-reliant. They aren't so proud and self-sufficient, thinking they can live without God or without His Word and Spirit working in their lives.

5. God will use these "things" to make us more tender, sympathetic, and understanding of the hurts, bruises, and needs of others:

> "Who comforts us in all our tribulation, that we may be able to comfort those who are in any trouble, with the comfort with which we ourselves are comforted by God" (II Corinthians 1:4).

6. God will use these "things" to teach us deeper lessons about His own person. We learn about His:

a. Forgiveness
   b. Faithfulness (He doesn't forsake us)
   c. Omnipotence (as He keeps His promise)
   d. Omnipresence (as He draws near to comfort us)
   e. Tenderness
   f. Patience (bearing long with us in our failures)
   g. Provision

7. God uses these "things" to prepare us for Heaven. So often we are so earth bound that we do not have that joyful anticipation of the coming glory. But pain, suffering, sorrow and tragedy, etc. will develop a godly longing to be with Christ. Perhaps your heartaches are preparing you to look up, for your redemption is drawing nigh.

In Romans 8:23-27 we see that many times our experience in life is filled with sighs, tears, and groans. We often don't know how to pray, "For we do not know what we should pray for as we ought." (verse 26). But we draw the contrast between what we don't know in verse 26, and what we do know in verse 28: "We know all things work together for good." William Cowper, the great English hymn writer, expresses our feelings very well:

God moves in a mysterious way
His wonders to perform;
He plants His footsteps in the sea,
And rides upon the storm.

Deep in unfathomable mines
Of never failing skill
He treasures up His bright designs,
And works His sovereign will.

Ye fearful saints, fresh courage take;
The clouds ye so much dread
Are big with mercy, and shall break
In blessings on your head.

Judge not the Lord by feeble sense,
But trust Him for His grace;
Behind a frowning providence
He hides a smiling face.

His purposes will ripen fast,
Unfolding ev'ry hour;
The bud may have a bitter taste,
But sweet will be the flow'r.

Blind unbelief is sure to err,
And scan His work in vain;
God is His own interpreter,
And He will make it plain.

The late Dr. R. C. Sproul, theologian and author, commenting on this great promise from Paul, said:

> "Romans 8:28 is one of the most comforting texts in all of Scripture. It assures the believer that all 'tragedies' are ultimately blessings. It does not declare that all things that happen are good in themselves but that in all the things that happen to us God is working in and through them for our good. This is also firmly grounded in His eternal purpose for His people."[2]

4
Samson's Riddle

"Out Of The Eater, (Devourer) Came Forth Meat, And Out Of The Strong, (Bitter) Came Forth Sweetness." Judges 14:14

*L*ife is full of sorrows and sufferings. These are things that we cannot escape from in this fallen world. Every child of God has passed through the flame, through the desert, and through the painful experiences of life. Who can understand these crushing providences when they come crashing into our world? The hymn writer has expressed for us, in poetic verse, the mystery of sorrow, pain, and death that we often face in our daily lives.

"Not now, but in the coming years,
It may be in the better land,
We'll read the meaning of our tears,
And there, some time we'll understand.

We'll catch the broken thread again,
And finish what we here began;
Heaven will the mysteries explain,
And then, Ah then, we'll understand.

We'll know why clouds instead of sun
Were over many a cherished plan;
Why song has ceased when scarce begun;
Tis there some time, we'll understand.

Why what we long for most of all,
Eludes so oft our eager hand,
Why hopes are crushed and castles fall;
Up there, some time, we'll understand.

God knows the way, He holds the key,
He guides us with unerring hand;
Some time with tearless eyes we'll see,
Yes, up there, we'll understand.

Then trust in God thro' all the days;
Fear not, for He doth hold thy hand;
Though dark the way, still sing and praise,
Some time, some time, we'll understand."

—Maxwell N. Cornelius

By Robert L. Dickie

I think all of us at times have groaned under the weight of afflictions and have found ourselves grumbling to God about the unfolding of His providence in our lives.

When it comes to suffering and difficulties, it is important that Christians understand the nature of God's providence. Providence simply means that God has not abandoned His creation and left all events to unfold by chance. But rather, God governs His creation by His own council and will. Proverbs 16:9, "A man's heart deviseth his way: but the Lord directeth his steps." Proverbs 21:1, "The king's heart is in the hand of the Lord, as the rivers of water: he turneth it whithersoever he will." Proverbs 21:31, "The horse is prepared against the day of battle: but safety is of the Lord." and Ephesians 1:11, "In whom also we have obtained an inheritance, being predestined according to the purpose of him who worketh all things after the council of his own will." These are just a few verses that remind us of God's sovereign control of His created world. God is not the absentee god of the deists. Our God reigns. And as He reigns over His universe, He also reigns over us. There is not a detail of our lives or the least of all the moments of our existence that He is not governing and controlling. Peace for the believer comes when we can submit to this wonderful thought. Stephen Charnock, a great Puritan theologian once said:

"Now what greater comfort is there than this, that there is one who presides in the world who is so wise he cannot be mistaken, so faithful he cannot deceive, so pitiful he cannot neglect his people, and so powerful that he can make stones even to be turned into bread if he please."

Such a God is truly a God of comfort and peace to His people.

The context of the story before us is this: the story of Samson takes place during the days of the judges. Israel had no king. Israel was a theocratic state where God was their ruler. He would raise up judges, or deliverers, to deliver the nation from her enemies. Samson, while going down to Timnath, slays a lion. Later, when he returns to view the dead lion, he finds a swarm of bees have made a nest inside the carcass of the dead animal. At a certain feast, Samson gave all of his guests a riddle. He said, "Out of the eater (literally one who devours) came forth meat, and out of the strong (literally bitter) came forth sweetness."

The answer to the riddle for us is simple to interpret since we have the story before us to read and to understand. The lion is the one who devours, but in this case, the lion yielded food. The lion is strong and would ruin many a person's hopes and dreams by destroying either life or property, but in this case the lion yielded sweetness, the honey that Samson had found in the lion's carcass.

I believe this riddle has a special spiritual lesson for all of us to learn. Out of the devouring and bitter experiences of life, come the sweetest lessons, and the most precious times that we ever have with the Lord. Let me give you the universal principle of Samson's riddle, "Out of the eater, (devourer) came forth meat, and out of the strong, (bitter) came forth sweetness." There are three things that I want to share with you from this text. First, this principle is illustrated in the Bible. Second, this principle is illustrated in the world of nature. And third, this principle is illustrated in our own lives.

This Principle Is Illustrated In The Bible

First, we have the example of Joseph. Twenty years after Joseph was betrayed by his brothers, he meets them and tells them, "Ye thought evil against me but God meant it for good." Genesis 50:20. Joseph's brothers sold him as a slave; this was a terrible and bitter experience. Joseph's greatest honor arose out of his deepest sorrows! In Potiphar's prison he never dreamed he would one day be next to Pharaoh in power and authority in all of Egypt.

Second, we have the example of Job, "The Lord gave and the Lord taketh away." Job 1:21. Job lost everything he had and experienced the most crushing of life's disappointments one after the other, only to find God's special favor upon him, and to later receive more than he ever lost. Job did not say, "The Lord gave but the devil hath taken away." All of the bitter moments of life can be made sweet when we believe a smiling providence is behind them all.

"God moves in a mysterious way
His wonders to perform
He plants His footsteps in the sea,
And rides upon the storm.

You fearful saints, fresh courage take;
The clouds you so much dread,
Are big with mercy and shall break.
With blessings on your head.

Judge not the Lord by feeble sense,
But trust Him for His grace;
Behind a frowning providence,
He hides a smiling face.

His purposes will ripen fast,
Unfolding every hour,
The bud may have a bitter taste;
But sweet will be the flower.

Blind unbelief is sure to err,
And scan His work in vain;
God is His own interpreter,
And He will make it plain."

—William Cowper, 1774

Third, we have the example of David when he said in his Psalm, "Before I was afflicted I went astray, but now I have kept Thy word." Psalm 119:67. The old Puritan writer David Dickson once said, "When prosperity is abused, it is God's mercy to us, to visit us with the rod of affliction, and by it to drive us to make better use of His word."[1] David's afflictions may have been the trials and tragedies after his sin with Bathsheba. David lost a son, and later lost a nation. Calvin once said, "Experience demonstrates that so long as God deals gently with us, we are always breaking forth into insolence." (insolence meaning bold, presumptuous, reckless, and insulting behavior.)

Fourth, we have the example of Jeremiah. After King Nebuchadnezzar captured Jerusalem, the Lord appeared to Jeremiah and revealed a vision of two baskets of figs (Jeremiah 24:1-5). The Lord asked Jeremiah if he knew what these figs represented. The two baskets of figs were quite different from each other. One basket of figs was ripe and good; the other basket of figs was filled with rotten figs that could not be eaten. These two baskets of figs represented the people of Israel. There were two different groups of people in Israel: those carried away into captivity, and those who remained in the land. We would expect the basket of figs that was rotten represented the bad people who were carried away into captivity, while the good basket of figs represented the people who were allowed to remain in the land. But we are wrong!

The Lord Himself tells Jeremiah what the two baskets of figs represent. The good basket of figs represents the people who were carried away to Babylon, God says, "For their good." And the Lord says He will, "give them an heart to know me, that I am the Lord: and they shall be my people, and I will be their God: for they shall return unto me with their whole heart." And the evil or bad figs represented the people who remained in the land. They will be judged and will not have the blessing of the Lord. The vision of Jeremiah illustrates how God's ways and God's thoughts are not our ways or our thoughts.

Fifth, we have the example of Peter. His denial of Christ and subsequent repentance taught him some of his most important lessons in his Christian walk. Peter wrote:

> "Wherein ye greatly rejoice, though now for a season, if need be, ye are in heaviness through manifold temptations: that the trial of your faith, being much more precious than of gold that perisheth, though it be tried with fire, might be found unto praise and honour and glory at the appearing of Jesus Christ."

I Peter 1:6-7. Peter could only say this because of the bitter experience he endured after Gethsemane. My dear friends, let us not complain if we are in the fiery furnace of affliction being purified by fire.

Sixth, we have the example of Paul the Apostle. Here is God's great champion. Paul is given a thorn in the flesh to prepare him for future ministry. He writes about this experience in II Cor. 12:7-10:

> "And lest I should be exalted above measure through the abundance of the revelations, there was given to me a thorn in the flesh, the messenger of Satan to buffet me, lest I should be exalted above measure, For this thing I besought the Lord thrice, that it might depart from me. And He said unto me, My grace is sufficient for thee: for my strength is made perfect in weakness. Most gladly therefore will I rather glory in my infirmities, that the power of Christ may rest upon me. Therefore I take pleasure in infirmities, in reproaches, in necessities, in persecutions, in distresses for Christ's sake: for when I am weak, then am I strong."

Seventh, we have the example of Naomi in the Old Testament book of Ruth. Naomi's son married Ruth, a Moabitess. This marriage was contrary to the revealed will of God. To the Jews this was a great sin (a Jew marrying a Gentile). And yet, by God's providence this was over ruled. This Gentile woman, Ruth, was brought to a place where she would choose God to be her God, and Israel to be her people. "Your people shall be my people and your God shall be my God." Ruth 1:16. When Naomi's son died, Ruth remarried Boaz and she found herself in the lineage of Jesus Christ! Matthew 1:5. So God is able to overrule our sins to bring good into our lives. This does not mean we should sin that good may come of it. This simply encourages us that even when we fail all is not lost.

Finally, we have the example of Jesus our Lord. Out of the bitter loneliness and agony of Gethsemane and Calvary came the sweet grace of redemption.

Summary

The Scriptures reveal the devouring and bitter experiences of life produce our greatest lessons and blessings. "Out of the eater came forth meat, and out of the strong came forth sweetness." To learn from these experiences, as we do from all the lessons of life, we must be willing to meditate on the precious Word of God. Puritan Thomas Brooks once said: "It is not he who reads most, but he who meditates most... who will prove to be the choicest, sweetest, wisest, and strongest Christian!"[2] Martin Luther also agreed that the greatest spiritual lessons we learn in life come from our experience with God in the trials and tribulations. Luther said, "I never knew the meaning of God's word until I came into affliction."[3] There is no better school to learn the things of God than the School of the Spirit.

This Principle Is Illustrated In The World Of Nature

First, we have the lesson from the farmer's seed. The seed must die in order for life and fruit to be brought forth. "Except a corn of wheat fall into the ground and die, it abideth alone: but if it die, it bringeth forth much fruit." John 12:24. Death must take place before there can be the miracle of life. Is it not amazing that from death comes life? Second, we have the lesson from the caterpillar that it must die for the beautiful butterfly to emerge. Third, the baby eaglet, so dependent upon its mother, would never learn to soar in the majestic and lofty heights unless forced and rudely pushed from its nest so it could learn to fly on its own. It must face fear and uncertainty to experience flight. Fourth, the oyster has its world painfully altered by the intrusion of one tiny grain of sand. The sand is painful, it scratches, it annoys, and it causes irritation. What does the oyster do? Well, what do most of us do when something painful, irritating, or annoying comes into our lives? Usually we complain, we murmur, we decide God is unfair or unjust, and we become atheists or agnostics. We might pretend that these painful, irritating, and annoying things do not really exist! Or, we could humbly accept them as God's will for us and try to bear up cheerfully and patiently until God reveals to us His secret purpose! And should God never choose to reveal why we suffer, we must still humbly worship Him with the attitude that says, "Be still and know that I am God." What does the oyster do with the tiny grain of irritating sand? It begins to work with the unfriendly irritant. It covers the grain of sand with one coat after another of a milky substance until finally the pearl is made! Someone has said, the pearl is, "A thing of wondrous beauty wrapped around trouble." Even in the world of nature we learn that, "Out of the eater came forth meat, and out of the strong came forth sweetness."

This Principle Is Illustrated In Our Own Lives

Life's greatest lessons are learned in the midst of our deepest sorrows. In my many years of pastoral experience I do not hesitate to say that the greatest lessons I have learned in life were learned in the school of the Spirit where I learned to walk with God in the valleys of suffering. By grace, my God has taught me, "Whatever my lot, He has taught me to say, it is well, it is well with my soul!" I would also venture to say that the pain, suffering, sorrow, and death you have experienced in life has had a more profound impact on you than any other earthly teacher. The Holy Spirit uses these kinds of things to mold and shape us into the image of Christ. There was a dear lady who came to a Bible study at our church a few years back. Her name was Lily Sharp. Lily's story was printed in a Christian magazine. I think her story illustrates Samson's riddle powerfully.

Lily's Story

Lily grew up very poor. Her parents didn't love her or want her. As a little girl she recalls how her parents would leave at night to go out drinking, partying, and leave her home alone crying and afraid. At nine years of age she was hired out to clean houses, and at twelve years of age she was put in an institution for unwanted children. Here she was separated from her little sister whom she raised herself.

Desperately seeking love and acceptance, she married at sixteen, and for the next thirty years she lived with an abusive husband. Lily came to know the Lord and prayed desperately for a miracle to heal her marriage.

One day she was heading up North to get away for some rest when something tragic happened. Her twenty-year-old son, Scott, was in a terrible automobile accident, and the doctors said he would never survive. Instead of sending a miracle to heal her marriage, the

Lord sent a terrible disaster into her life. After all she had been through, did she really need this? But who are we to question God? Was God being cruel and unfair? Later Lily herself said, "God uses hurts to make you strong so you can do something for others who are hurting the same way."

Her son Scott lived. He cannot walk, talk, and is confined to a wheelchair. Scott can communicate only through a specially built computer. Through this experience, Scott became a believer, and with his mother's help and his computer, he supports 100 children ($2,000 per month) so they can have food and an education, and he corresponds regularly with them by computer, writing to share God's love with them!

Yes indeed, "Out of the eater came forth meat, and out of the bitter came forth sweetness." I have three questions to ask each of you who are reading this:

1. How do you handle troubles and sorrows? We must handle them the same way we do when we read signs along the highway when we travel that tell us to "Beware of falling rocks!" Like falling rocks, many troubles cannot be avoided. (How do you miss a falling rock?) We can only submit to God's will and accept these unexpected troubles as well as we can if they happen to us.

2. How can we explain suffering, pain, disappointments, and death? In the context of the fall. In the context of God's providence, Romans 8:28. In the context of time! No one would complain if God allowed just one moment of suffering during a lifetime of comfort. Why then should we complain if we face a lifetime of suffering, which is but a moment in contrast to eternity? Looking at our troubles, sorrows, and disappointments in the light of eternity makes them appear very small indeed!

3. What lessons can we learn from Samson's riddle? First, "In everything give thanks." I Thessalonians 5:18. Second, "All things work together for good." Romans 8:28. When Horatio Spafford learned in 1873 that his four daughters had perished in a terrible accident at sea, he was devastated and crushed. But in his sorrow he knew that God was still on the throne. In beautiful submission to God, he wrote that famous hymn, "It Is Well With My Soul."

"When peace like a river attendeth my way,
When sorrows like sea billows roll;
Whatever my lot, Thou hast taught me to say,
It is well, it is well, with my soul!"

One Christian writer commented on this lesson:

> "The diamond must be cut to bring out its beauty, the gold must be refined to bring out its purity, the vine must be pruned that it may bear more fruit, the clay must be molded that it might become a vessel fit for use, and the child of God must be cut and refined and pruned and molded that he might become fit for the Master's use. It seems sometimes the clay will be ruined in the molding, but the purpose of the Potter is the object of molding; do not flinch, do not resist, pray."[4]

Once again, let me repeat our text, "Out of the eater came forth meat, and out of the bitter came forth sweetness." Judges 14:14

By Robert L. Dickie

5
"...So Great Salvation"
Hebrews 2:3

(Encouragement for those who think they are too sinful to be saved)

Our text tells us that salvation is a great salvation. It's not just a good salvation, an adequate salvation, or a sufficient salvation. It is called a great salvation. It is great in the fact that a great God planned it and provided it. It is great in that it is far superior to any other way that man may try to follow in order to get to heaven. It is great in that it cost God everything but costs the humble believer nothing. It is great in that it does in fact accomplish all that it sets out to do.

Our text tells us that God saves. What does He save us from? We are saved from the power of sin, the guilt of sin, the fear of sin's consequences. I John 4:18,

"There is no fear in love, but perfect love casts out fear, because fear involves torment. But he who fears has not been made perfect in love."

Our text asks the question, "How shall we escape if we neglect so great salvation?"

An old Puritan commented on this thought of escaping the wrath of God if we neglect this great salvation:

> "How shall we escape if we neglect so great salvation? That is, if we, through carelessness or stubbornness, neglect to make our calling and election sure? If we trample underfoot the Son of GOD, His Love in dying for us, and esteem His precious Blood with which He seals His covenant an unholy, or common thing? The greater the Salvation is, the more grievous will the Damnation of those be who neglect it. Nothing can possibly provoke the LORD GOD more than that Men should slight His mercy, which He has so stupendously and wonderfully manifested in CHRIST His Son. The Son must also be angry that after all He has done for His vineyard, men should make light of His love, which He has shewed in dying for them. But to explain this point more particularly, it is necesary to shew that impenitent sinners of every kind do not and cannot escape the vengeance of God."[1]

By Robert L. Dickie

I'm writing to the one who is doubting his salvation. You have great sins in your past. You feel that because of these sins and failures you cannot enter heaven. You believe these sins will prevent you from entering the Kingdom of God. You wish you could erase them all. You grieve that you committed such acts of rebellion and treason against the Lord. Because of these sins, you have concluded that God would never save someone like you; therefore, you have lost all hope of going to heaven and being with Christ.

But, dear friend, did Christ die for only the perfect? Did Christ die only for those with little sins or few sins? Did Christ die only for "good" sinners but "bad" sinners He cannot save? If you could erase all the sins you recall in your past, would that make you any more lovable to God? What did the Apostle Paul say? "But God commendeth His love toward us, in that while we were yet sinners, Christ died for us." Romans 5:8. Jesus died for sinners, not for those who were righteous and good. No man is worthy of salvation. Again Paul says, "For all have sinned and come short of the glory of God." Romans 3:23.

My friend, how can you refuse to believe what the Savior has said to us all? "Come unto Me, all ye that labor and are heavy laden, and I will give you rest." Matthew 11:28. Is this not a gracious invitation for someone precisely like you? You are burdened over your sin. You mourn that you committed those sins. You would die a thousand deaths to rid yourself of these sins if you could. Just as Jesus said, because of these sins in your past, you are laboring under an enormous weight of guilt, conviction, shame, and sorrow. You stagger daily at the weight of your spiritual burden. How is it that you cannot see that the Savior's words were intended for someone just like you? "Come unto Me all ye that labor and are heavy laden, and I will give you rest." Why do you refuse to see this?

Again I ask you, "Did Jesus die only for sinners who weren't too bad? Or did He die for great sinners, for big sinners, for sinners like you, who feel there is no hope for them? The blood of Jesus Christ, shed on the cross, atones for all our sins. Jesus is the sinner's hope. Jesus is the sinner's refuge. Jesus is the sinner's hiding place. My friend, have you forgotten this?

Is Jesus not big enough, gracious enough, loving enough, kind enough, that He cannot save a sinner like you? Do not lose sight of what a great Savior He is! As the Apostle Paul said, "How shall we escape if we neglect so great salvation?" Hebrews 2:3. Jesus has provided not just any salvation, the apostle tells us it is a great salvation.

Jesus is the friend of sinners. Jesus is the only hope for sinners. Jesus is the rest for sinners. Jesus is the peace for sinners. Jesus is the hiding place for sinners. As the Bible says, Jesus is the rock cleft for you! The hymn writer said it so well:

By Robert L. Dickie

"Rock of ages, cleft for me,
Let me hide myself in thee,
Let the water and the blood,
From Thy wounded side that flowed,
Be of sin the double cure,
Save from wrath and make me pure."

My dear friend, you think your sins are too great and that God would never pardon you. You think you cannot be forgiven. But your Savior has provided for you a hiding place in the "clefts of the rock." As it says in the Song of Solomon 2:14, Jesus is that cleft Rock. Jesus is that hiding place. When Satan condemns you, chastens you, rebukes you, and accuses you, then run to Jesus by faith. Run to Him! Trust in His blood. Rejoice in His righteousness. And hear Jesus say to your weary heartbroken soul:

"O My dove, that art in the clefts of the rock, in the secret places of the stairs, let me see thy countenance, let Me hear thy voice, for sweet is thy voice, and thy countenance is comely." Song of Solomon 2:14

My friend, your Savior has provided you a hiding place. A dove is a helpless bird when hunted by the eagle or the hawk. The only hope he has is to fly to the rocky cliffs and hide in one of the many crevices or clefts and there find safety from the clutches of the eagle. The sinner is the dove. The cleft of the rock is Jesus our hiding place. Just as the dove finds shelter from the birds of prey in the clefts of the rock, so too the sinner finds safety from the judgment in the Lord Jesus Christ. Jesus Himself is the secret stairway to Heaven. His love for you is so great that He invites you to approach Him. He desires to hear your voice in prayer and worship. He tells you the very sight of you is precious to His eyes.

The Lord is your hiding place. He is your refuge where you can run and find safety, forgiveness, acceptance, peace, pardon, adoption, fellowship, friendship, sonship, and a host of other blessings too wonderful to fully comprehend.

So, my dear friend, how can you despair and feel as if there is no hope for you? Has He not invited you, a great sinner, to come to Him? And did He not say, "… and him that cometh to Me I will in no wise cast out"? John 6:37. Why can't you trust Jesus to do what He says He will do if you come to Him? Come to Him and He will not cast you out.

Friend, it is Satan who whispers in your ears that Jesus will not forgive you. It is Satan who seeks to rob you of joy, peace, rest, and happiness. Jesus said in John 10:10, "The thief cometh not but for to steal, and to kill, and to destroy…." Satan is that thief who comes to do these things. But Jesus came, "…that they might have life, and that they might have it more abundantly." Remember, my dear friend, the words of the Apostle Paul, "In whom we have redemption through His blood, the forgiveness of sins, according to the riches of His grace." Ephesians 1:7. Redemption is the act of being purchased out of the slave market of sin. The price of your redemption (purchase) was the precious blood of Christ. Peter tells us:

> "Knowing that you were not redeemed with corruptible things, like silver or gold, from your aimless conduct received by tradition from your fathers, but with the precious blood of Christ, as of a lamb without blemish and without spot." I Peter 1:18-19.

When you were a slave, trapped in the spiritual world of darkness, dead in trespasses and sins, Jesus came and paid to set you free. The purchase price was His life and death.

When you allow the devil to fill your heart and mind with doubts, you are falling into the same trap God's people fell into during the days of the Babylonian captivity. The Babylonian captives doubted God's love and forgot His kindness and grace. To a despondent people in captivity, God commanded them to sing and to worship Him. But they refused because of their lack of faith. God said to them, "Sing O heavens and be joyful O earth...." "But Zion said, the Lord hath forsaken me, and my Lord hath forgotten me." O, but notice God's response to their despair! God uses the analogy of a nursing mother with a newborn baby to make His point that He will never forsake those who trust in Him.

> "Can a woman forget her sucking child, that she should not have compassion on the son of her womb? Yea, they may forget yet will I not forget thee. Behold, I have graven thee on the palms of my hands; thy walls are continually before me." Isaiah 49:15-16.

It is highly unlikely that a mother would forget or neglect her newborn baby that she nurses on her breast. But even if some mother would be so hard and unloving to do that, God says He will never forsake His people who have put their trust in Him. The hymn writer put it this way:

"My name from the Palms of His hands
Eternity cannot erase,
Impressed on His heart it remains,
With marks of indelible grace."

My dear weary, depressed, and despondent friend. I beg of you to look to Christ! He is our only hope. "Looking unto Jesus the author and finisher of our faith." Hebrews 12:1. Do not look to your past. Do not look to your sins. Do not look to your feelings or your failures. If you look there, you will be filled with despair. Just look to Jesus by faith. Lift up your eyes and look to Him. Jesus is our hiding place. Jesus is our fountain filled with blood. Jesus is our mercy seat.

Jesus is our hiding place:

Hail Sovereign Love
By Jehoiada Brewer

Hail sovereign love that first began,
The scheme to rescue fallen man.
Hail matchless, free, eternal grace,
That gave my soul a hiding place.

Against the God who rules the sky,
I fought with hand uplifted high;
Despised the mention of His grace,
Too proud to seek a hiding place.

Enwrapped in thick Egyptian night,
And fond of darkness more than light;
Madly I ran the sinful race,
Secure without a hiding place.

But thus the eternal counsel ran,
"Almighty love, arrest that man!"
I felt the arrows of disgrace,
And found I had no hiding place.

Indignant Justice stood in view,
To Sinai's fiery mount I flew.
But Justice cried with frowning face,
This mountain is no hiding place.
Ere long an angel's voice I heard,
And Mercy's angel face appeared.
She led me on with placid pace,
To Jesus as my hiding place.

Should storms of sevenfold thunders roll,
And shake the globe from pole to pole.
No flaming bolt shall daunt my face,
For Jesus is my hiding place.

On Him, eternal judgment fell,
That must have sunk a world to Hell,
He bore it for the chosen race,
And thus became their hiding place.

A few more rolling suns at most,
Shall land my soul on Canaan's coast.
Where I shall sing the songs of grace,
And gaze upon my hiding place!

By Robert L. Dickie

Jesus is our fountain filled with blood:

There is a Fountain Filled With Blood

There is a fountain filled with blood,
Drawn from Emmanuel's veins;
And sinners plunged beneath that flood
Lose all their guilty stains.

The dying thief rejoiced to see
that fountain in his day;
And there have I, though vile as he,
washed all my sins away.

Dear dying Lamb, Thy precious blood
shall never lose its power
Till all the ransomed church of God
be saved, to sin no more.

E'er since, by faith, I saw the stream
Thy flowing wounds supply,
Redeeming love has been my theme,
and shall be till I die.

Then in a nobler, sweeter song,
I'll sing Thy power to save,
When this poor lisping, stammering tongue
lies silent in the grave.

Jesus is our mercy seat:

Approach My Soul The Mercy Seat

Approach my soul, the mercy seat,
Where Jesus answers prayer;
There humbly fall before His feet,
For none can perish there.

Thy promise is my only plea;
With this I venture nigh:
Thou callest burdened souls to Thee,
And such, O Lord, Am I.

Bowed down beneath a load of sin,
By Satan sorely pressed,
By wars without, and fears within,
I come to Thee for rest.

Be Thou my shield and hiding place,
That sheltered near thy side,
I may my fierce accuser face,
And tell him, Thou hast died.

O, wondrous love! To bleed and die,
To bear the cross and shame,
That guilty sinners, such as I,
Might plead Thy gracious Name! Amen.

—John Newton, 1779
CM

By Robert L. Dickie

Dear struggling, doubting friend, let us be clear about sin. All sin is a violation of the holy laws of God. Sin is willful treason and rebellion against the High King of Heaven. Sin is an insult to our Creator. All sin must be confessed and repented of. Why? Because "For the wages of sin is death but the gift of God is eternal life through Jesus Christ our Lord." Romans 6:23.

So you feel you cannot be forgiven. Did Jesus not come to save sinners? An angel, in a dream, appeared and told Joseph, the husband of Mary "And He (Jesus) shall save His people from their sins." Matthew 1:21. Yes, Jesus will save His people from their sins. If you are brokenhearted over your sins, if you have turned from them and have forsaken them, why would the Savior not do what He has promised and forgive you? John tells us, "If we confess our sins He is faithful and just to forgive us of our sins and to cleanse us from all unrighteousness." I John 1:9. Paul told the Philippian jailor in Acts 16:31, "...believe on the Lord Jesus Christ and thou shalt be saved."

My dear friend, the very fact that you mourn over your sins and failures, that you confess them and repent of them, is an indication that the Lord has worked in your heart. Be encouraged by these signs. If you had no desire to be forgiven or free from the lusts of your flesh, you would have reason to be alarmed at the condition of your soul.

God Himself has invited sinners like us to come and reason with Him. In Isaiah 1:18 the Lord says, "Come now, and let us reason together, saith the Lord: though your sins be as scarlet, they shall be white as snow; though they be red like crimson, they shall be as wool."

I invite you to come to Jesus with all your sins, with all your guilt, with all your sorrows and shame. And by one act of faith, roll this entire burden upon the Lord Jesus Christ. Jesus died for sinners and to sinners He says, "I am the way, the truth, and the life. No man cometh unto the Father but by Me." John 14:6.

Jesus is the doorway to heaven. Jesus is the path that leads to the Father. Jesus is the way, the truth, and the life. My dear friend, throw yourself by faith into the arms of Jesus. If you perish, perish there. But I remind you that no one who has ever come to Jesus in faith with repentance was turned away. So lay your sins on Jesus. Confess them and bring them to Him. The hymn writer makes this point crystal clear:

I lay my sins on Jesus,
The spotless Lamb of God,
He bears them all and frees us
From the accursed load.

I bring my guilt to Jesus,
To wash my crimson stains,
White in His blood most precious,
Till not a spot remains.

Jesus died and paid the price for all our sins. Jesus has promised a great salvation. It is great in its design. God designed His salvation to save sinners, even great sinners. It is great in its accomplishment. When Christ said on the cross, "It is finished," He accomplished your salvation. It is complete. It is finished. It's done and paid for. The salvation that Jesus provided is great enough and big enough to save every sinner, big or small, from all their sins. Jesus lived the life you could not live and He died the death you should have died. Therefore, my friend, come to Jesus. Come and find that His love and His grace is big enough and great enough for a sinner like you. O the life Christ lived! So pure, so holy, so perfect! And O the death Christ died! Dying for every sin we ever committed. Dying for our every word, thought, or deed that violated the law of His Father. Trust that life and that death. It is the finished work of Christ in His living and dying that saves us from all our sins, even our big sins. Hallelujah! What a Savior!

Yes, we have a great salvation. Dr. Martyn Lloyd-Jones commented on why the salvation we have in Christ is so great. The good doctor says:

> "In this modern world there is nothing quite so wonderful as this 'so great salvation' (Hebrews 2:3). What is comparable to the knowledge of sins forgiven? What is more wonderful than to be able to put your head on the pillow, knowing that if you

die during the night it doesn't matter, knowing that you have already passed from judgment to life and that you will go to heaven and wake up there as a child of God? Oh, how wonderful is the companionship of Christ.

But there is something still more wonderful—the world to come. This world is a doomed world. It is a sinful world, and the New Testament does not offer to make it better. In fact it tells us that it will get worse and worse. But it does offer us "new heavens and a new earth, wherein dwelleth righteousness" (2 Peter 3:13)."[2]

By Robert L. Dickie

6
Discovering the Peace of Romans 8:28

"*I* must confess that I am driven to my knees by the overwhelming conviction that I have no where else to go. My wisdom and that of all about me is insufficient to meet the demands of the day.

—Abraham Lincoln

"And we know that all things work together for good to them that love God, to them who are the called according to his purpose." Romans 8:28

One of the most comforting verses in the Bible is found in Paul's letter to the church at Rome. Romans 8:28 is one of the most well-loved and well-known verses in all the Scriptures. This verse has been a great comfort to the people of God through the ages. I have made reference to this verse throughout this book. Here it is once again. "And we know that all things work together for good to them that love God, to them who are the called according to his purpose."

Often people will ask me, "How does this verse really work?" The phrase "All things" refers to everything that may happen in our lives whether it is good or bad. How can all things be good for us? Does this mean that even disappointments, tragedies, failures, heartaches, and sorrows are good for us? The answer is yes. Romans 8:28 is essential to a biblical worldview. Let me share with you some of the lessons I have learned over the years that relate to this precious promise from the Word of God. God uses "all things" good or bad:

1. To get our attention and draw us into His arms.

2. To develop patience in our lives.

3. To teach us to pray and to trust Him.

4. To teach us humility.

5. To make us tender, sympathetic, and understanding of others when they too go through tough and difficult times.

6. To teach us about God's patience and faithfulness.

7. To prepare us for heaven. Most of us are too earthbound and content to be here below. Sufferings and trials shake us loose of time and life and create a longing to be home with the Lord.

British author, Sharon James, understands that God often uses unusual circumstances and hard providences to teach His children some of their most important lessons. Here are some of her comments on this subject:

"The Lord's priorities are so different from ours! God didn't just want to take the people to the land of milk and honey as quickly as possible. That was what they wanted, of course. No, God wanted them to increase in faith and trust. He wanted their holiness. It is just the same for us. God's priority is not for us to get through life as easily and comfortably as we can. Humanly speaking, that's just what we want! But his purpose is for us to become like Christ. Sometimes he leads us into hard places, where it may seem as if he has abandoned us. All too often we reason: "Because my life is so unbearable at the moment, the Lord must have forgotten me!" But sometimes the Lord does deliberately lead us to these hard places. We then learn to rely utterly on him."[1]

Corrie Ten Boom, a woman who suffered intensely under Nazi rule in Germany, often quoted this wonderful poem that reminded her that God was involved in all the things that happen in our lives, whether good or bad, to mold us into the image of His Son:

My life is but a weaving between my Lord and me.
I cannot choose the colors, He weaveth steadily.
Oft times He weaveth sorrow, and I in foolish pride,
Forget He sees the upper, but I the underside.
Not till the looms are silent and the shuttles cease to fly,
Will God unroll the canvas and explain the reasons why.
The dark threads are just as needful in the Weaver's skillful hands.
As the threads of gold and silver in the patterns He has planned.

—Grant Colfax Tuller

Why is Romans 8:28 so important to us as we consider this subject of developing a biblical worldview for Christian living? It is for this one significant reason: we believe in the absolute sovereignty of God in all things. This great God, who chose, called, and regenerated us, also determines all things in our lives. We are to see ourselves as people of destiny. We should see ourselves as people who have been made in the image of God. Because of this, we should, of all people, strive for success. But having done all we can to achieve our goals, we should then leave the results in His sovereign hands. Not everyone will win the race; not everyone will reach the target they are aiming for; not everyone can be the biggest or the best. But we will never achieve anything if we don't have a goal, if we don't set our sights on higher things. As I would train my children in their athletic competitions, I would ask them, "What is your goal? What do you want to accomplish?" Once we establish that, we can begin careful planning to seek to reach and achieve those goals. We first start by seeing what our end or destination is. Then we devise a plan. We set smaller achievable goals in front of us first. Then we see what sacrifices we need to make to reach these lesser goals. There is an old saying, "Rome was not built in a day." So, with hard work, sacrifice, and patience, we pursue our dreams. We may not always reach what we aimed at, but I'll tell you what — you will reach a lot higher and go a lot further if you set out to reach those goals than if you don't do this at all. If you shoot for the moon, you may not hit the moon, but you will shoot a lot higher than if you only shot at the tops of the trees.

Romans 8:28 brings peace to the lives of those who have followed Christ through the years with a passion to know and serve Him. How wonderful to come to the end of life and have that confidence that you have done your best to honor and serve God! E. Stanley Jones, the Methodist missionary and evangelist who spent over fifty years of his life serving God in the Indian sub-continent, came to the end of his life and wrote these inspiring words:

> There are scars on my faith, but underneath those scars there are no doubts. [Christ] has me with the consent of all my being and with the cooperation of all my life. The song I sing is a lit song. Not the temporary exuberance of youth that often fades when middle and old age sets in with their disillusionment and cynicism...no, I'm 83, and I'm more excited today about being a Christian than I was at 18 when I first put my feet upon the way.[2]

George Matheson expresses something very similar to this thought in his book *Thoughts for Life's Journey*. Matheson, like E. Stanley Jones, knew that God's hard providences provide the best school of preparation for His servants. Matheson writes:

> My soul, reject not the place of thy prostration! It has ever been thy robbing-room for royalty. Ask the great ones of the past what has been the spot of their prosperity; they will say, "It was the cold ground on which I once was lying." Ask Abraham; he will point you to the sacrifice on Moriah. Ask Joseph; he will direct you to his dungeon. Ask Moses; he will date his fortune from his danger in the Nile. Ask Ruth; she will bid you build her monument in the field of her toil. Ask David; he will tell you

that his songs come from the night. Ask Job; and he will remind you that God answered him out of the whirlwind. Ask Peter; he will extol his submersion in the sea. Ask John; he will give the palm to Patmos. Ask Paul; he will attribute his inspiration to the light which struck him blind. Ask one more — the Son of Man. Ask Him whence has come His rule over the world. He will answer, "From the cold ground on which I was lying — the Gethsemane ground; I received My scepter there." Thou too, my soul, shalt be garlanded by Gethsemane. The cup thou fain wouldst pass from thee will be thy coronet in the sweet by-and-by. The hour of thy loneliness will crown thee. The day of thy depression will regale thee. It is thy desert that will break forth into singing; it is the trees of thy silent forest that will clap their hands... The voice of God to thine evening will be this, "Thy treasure is hid in the ground where thou wert lying."[3]

As we grow old in life, we see so many things changing around us. The years come and go, good friends pass away and go to be with the Lord, and we find we have so many more aches and pains. Growing old can be a fearful and dreadful experience for many people. Yet this ought not to be the case for those who know the Lord of the universe as their Savior, Friend, and everpresent Comforter. Romans 8:28 brings us peace when we realize that God is with us:

He has sustained us through all these many years, and as we see the shadows of death approaching, He will surely see us through to the other side. What great peace belongs to the one who has trusted God and walked with Him through the years! No child of God should approach death and old age with fear and trepidation. Keep your eyes on the Lord. Remind yourself that He has never failed you. As you journey through life, never forget that at every stage, the best is always yet to come.

The great hymn writer John Newton understood this. John Newton is most famous for writing the words to the beloved hymn "Amazing Grace." In a letter to one of his friends, Newton made this comment on Romans 8:28:

> ...If all things are in his hand, if the very hairs of our head are numbered; if every event, great and small, is under the direction of his providence and purpose; and if he has a wise, holy, and gracious end in view, to which everything that happens is subordinate and subservient — then we have nothing to do, but with patience and humility to follow as he leads, and cheerfully to expect a happy issue... How happy are they who can resign all to him, see his hand in every dispensation, and believe that he chooses better for them than they possibly could for themselves.[4]

I have not forgotten this as I have sought to walk with God and serve Him in my ministry. O friend, the best is always yet to come. When we are lying on our deathbed, and our loved ones and family gather around, remember that soon the angels themselves will carry you to your Lord and Savior Jesus Christ. What joy and happiness awaits those who have served Him faithfully through the years. And if you have many regrets, then carry these to the One who is full of love and mercy, whose invitation is always open to you, and He will forgive and wipe away all the stains, guilt, and regrets of your past life. Find the joy of being covered in the righteousness of Christ, and find the peace that comes from knowing you have been washed pure and white in the precious blood of Jesus Christ your Lord.

Grow old along with me!
The best is yet to be,
The last of life, for which the first was made:
Our times are in His hand
Who saith, "A whole I planned,
Youth shows but half; trust God: see all nor be afraid!"

—Robert Browning, from the poem Rabbi Ben Ezra

By Robert L. Dickie

7
How Shall We Sing The Lord's Song In A Strange Land?
Psalm 137:4

The children of Israel experienced an unusual providence. Judah, the southern kingdom, was invaded by the Babylonian empire, and the capital, Jerusalem, was sacked. The city was destroyed, millions of people were killed or taken away into slavery, and the kingdom was obliterated. Those who were carried away into Babylon were filled with deep grief and sorrow. Their hearts were broken; their dreams were shattered; their world was turned upside down; and their hopes for a future filled with joy, peace, hope and meaning was all but gone. While they languished in a strange land those who had taken them captive requested they sing some of the songs of Zion. These were the songs from their distant and destroyed homeland. With broken hearts and crushed spirits, the Psalmist captures the spirit of the people in Psalm 137. Here, in this Psalm, we have the essence of the deep pathos and sorrow of these languishing pilgrims who had been swept away to a far-off place. They are filled with such pain and disappointment that they are overflowing with both grief and sorrow. There is a haunting feeling hanging over the words of this Psalm. When we read these words we cannot but help feel drawn into the sorrows these dear people felt when asked to sing while they were beside the waters of the rivers of Babylon. Perhaps the story behind Psalm 137 has been used by the Lord over the years to bring comfort and joy to the people of God when they were languishing in a strange land and under a strange providence.

Read this Psalm and see if your heart is also touched and moved by the plight of these suffering Jews.

"By the rivers of Babylon, there we sat down, yea, we wept, when we remembered Zion. We hanged our harps upon the willows in the midst thereof. For there they that carried us away captive required of us a song; and they that wasted us required of us mirth, saying, Sing us one of the songs of Zion. How shall we sing the LORD's song in a strange land? If I forget thee, O Jerusalem, let my right hand forget her cunning. If I do not remember thee, let my tongue cleave to the roof of my mouth; if I prefer not Jerusalem above my chief joy. Remember, O LORD, the children of Edom in the day of Jerusalem; who said, Raze it, raze it, even to the foundation thereof. O daughter of Babylon, who art to be destroyed; happy shall he be, that rewardeth thee as thou hast served us. Happy shall he be, that taketh and dasheth thy little ones against the stones." Psalm 137

The author of this Psalm is unknown, and the time it was written is also uncertain. We know it was written during the Babylonian captivity of Judah or shortly afterward. The Babylonian captivity lasted for 70 years. Judah fell to the Babylonians around 586 B.C. This Psalm is one of the imprecatory Psalms. An imprecatory Psalm is one that pronounces a curse on the enemies of Jehovah and Israel. When we examine this Psalm, we need to see there are two applications and interpretations for this scripture. First, there is the historical message, which at face value gives us the meaning of the Psalm in a historical setting of Judah while in captivity. Second, there is a spiritual interpretation that applies to believers of all ages who find themselves in captivity to sin with its resulting consequences of sorrow, suffering, and separation from God. Augustine used this double application to be the foundation of his book, *The City of God*. In this book, Augustine drew a distinction between the city of God and the city of man.

I want to give a brief exposition of the historical nature of this Psalm. Then in the body of this message I will make the spiritual application to all of us who have known the struggle with the world, the flesh, and the devil.

The Exposition Of Psalm 137

Scottish Pastor Andrew Bonar made these comments on this Psalm of sorrow:

> "We feel it to be...strangely beautiful, full of pathos, and rising to sublimity; but what would be the fresh emotions of those who sang it first, and who dropped their tears into these rivers of Babel? No author's name is given; but so plaintive is it, that some have ascribed it to Jeremiah, the weeping prophet, of whose Lamentations it has been said, 'Every word seems written with a tear, and every sound seems the sob of a broken heart.'"[1]

In verses 1-4, we are given the sorrows and the tears of the exiles in Babylon:

> "By the rivers of Babylon, (The Euphrates and Tigris Rivers) there we sat down, yea, we wept, when we remembered Zion.(Zion refers in the historical sense to Jerusalem) We hanged our harps upon the

willows in the midst thereof. For there they (The Babylonians of King Nebuchadnezzar's armies) that carried us away captive required of us a song; and they that wasted us required of us mirth, saying, Sing us one of the songs of Zion. How shall we sing the LORD's song in a strange land?"

In verses 5-6 we are given the bitter memories these exiles have of their former state in Jerusalem and Judah. But now, with these painful memories, they languish and suffer in Babylon as captives in a strange land.

"If I forget thee, O Jerusalem, let my right hand forget her cunning. If I do not remember thee, let my tongue cleave to the roof of my mouth; if I prefer not Jerusalem above my chief joy."

This is referring to the historical setting that was part of the actual experience of the ancient Jews who suffered so terribly under the deprivations of Nebuchadnezzar's armies.

Verses 7-9 gives us the prayer and appeal to God to repay those responsible for their suffering and captivity:

"Remember, O LORD, the children of Edom (The Edomites were allies of the Babylonians and rejoiced in the persecution and captivity of the Jews) in the day of Jerusalem; who said, Raze it, raze it, even to the foundation thereof. (These Edomites seemed to be a cheering section egging the Babylonians on to do their evil work.) O daughter of Babylon, who art to be destroyed; happy shall he be, that rewardeth thee as thou hast served us. Happy shall he be, that taketh and dasheth thy little ones against the stones."

These last two verses are part of the imprecatory nature of this Psalm. Let me make some comments on these imprecatory Psalms:

1. These were written under the law and not under grace. In the New Covenant there is no equivalent to these imprecatory Psalms.

2. These Psalms display God's justice against the guilty and those who have sinned and rebelled against Him.

3. Sin brings consequences. Innocent children are often on the receiving end of their parents' sins and poor choices. Be careful how you live.

4. C.S. Lewis saw in this verse a spiritual lesson: little sins, little desires, begin so innocently. These little thoughts, ideas, indulgences, wants, and desires have small beginnings. But these little sins, if not dealt with firmly and courageously, will grow up to be monsters devouring

our lives. So, as C.S. Lewis said, "knock the little brat's brains out. And 'blessed' is he who can, for it is easier said than done." 2 Reflections, p. 113.

5. Spurgeon wrote, "Let those find fault with it who have never seen their temple burned, their city ruined, their wives ravished, and their children slain; they might not perhaps be so velvet-mouthed if they had suffered after this fashion. It is one thing to talk of the bitter feeling which moved captive Israelites in Babylon, and quite another thing to be captives ourselves under a strange and remorseless power, which knew not how to show mercy, but delighted in barbarities to the defenseless.... [Psalm 137] is a fruit of the captivity in Babylon, and often has it furnished expression for sorrows which else had been unutterable."[3]

Pastor James Montegomery Boice explained how he saw this Psalm:

1. The words are an appeal to God for justice. Here, as in each of the imprecatory psalms, the psalmist is not suggesting that he is about to take revenge on his enemies or even that he would if he could. On the contrary, he is appealing to God to do what is right and judge those who

have been excessively wicked and cruel in their actions. Derek Kidner says the first thing to notice about verses 7–9 is their "juridical background." The divine Judge is being presented with evidence against Edom and Babylon.

2. The judgments are only what God Himself decrees in other places. An entire book of the Bible was written to declare God's coming judgment on Edom. That book is Obadiah, and the reason given for the judgment is precisely what is alluded to in this psalm, namely, that when Jerusalem fell, the people of Edom did not mourn for their brother nation's suffering, as they should have, but rejoiced in the destruction instead. The prophet adds that the Edomites "stood aloof," "rejoice[d]," "seize[d] their wealth," and even "hand[ed] over the survivors" when they caught them (Obadiah 11–14). Other judgments on Edom may be found in Isaiah 34:5–15; 63:1–4; Jeremiah 49:7–22; Lamentations 4:21–22; Ezekiel 25:12–14; 35:1–15; 36:5; Joel 3:19; and Amos 1:11–12.

There are extensive prophecies against Babylon in Isaiah 13:1–14:23; 21:1–17; 47:1–15; and Jeremiah 50:1–51:64. Most telling is the account of the destruction of Mystery Babylon in Revelation 18 and 19. In those chapters the kings, merchants, sea captains, and other peoples of the earth mourn for the city. An angel joins in, and even the redeemed rejoice in God's judgment, crying, "Hallelujah!" as they praise God for it.

3. This is precisely what God has done. Romans 2:6 says that God "will give to each person according to what he has done" (citing Psalm 62:12; Proverbs 24:12). He has done it! Today the fortresses of ancient Edom are a desolate waste, and the site of ancient Babylon is a ruin. God cannot be mocked. "A man reaps what he sows" (Galatians 6:7), and "the one who sows to please his sinful nature, from that nature will reap destruction" (Galatians 6:8).[4]

I want to come to the spiritual side of this text and make our application to our lives from the spiritual lessons we can learn from this passage. The main theme of this text is the languishing of believers in a strange land. As we look at our text we will attempt to answer three questions:

1. What is this strange land?
2. How do believers get into this strange land?
3. How do believers get out of this strange land?

What Is This Strange Land?

The strange land represents a number of things. It can represent the state of being backslidden and out of fellowship with God. It can represent times of deep discouragement. It can represent times of loneliness and despair. It can represent times of doubts and fears.

Let me give you a survey of the words in this text:

- *Rivers* refers to the floods of sin, disobedience, doubts, trials and troubles

- *Babylon* refers to the world, or any place that is far from God. It also can represent a backslidden state.

- *Captive* refers to being bound by our sins, doubts, indifference and apathy, and our fears.

- *Wasted* refers to the toll that sin takes on a person's life. "The way of the transgressor is hard." Sin, fear, doubts, worries, and anxieties can all take a deadly toll on our lives.

- *Strange* reminds us this condition is no place for the people of God. "What doest thou here Elijah?" A Christian should not be in a state of fear, or a state of doubt, or a state of confusion, a state of spiritual deadness and backsliding, or in any kind of condition where we are far from God.

It was shocking to find that the people of God were in a strange land. They belonged in the land of promise. They belonged in the land flowing with milk and honey. These people lost their joy, song, way, hope, and their peace. Any of us can lose these things if we backslide. If we disobey the Lord, we may end up with sin, sorrow, discouragement, despair, or disappointments. The strange land is part of our experience in a fallen world. We can expect times like this on occasion. But we are more than conquerors through Him that loved us. Only in Christ can we be more than conquerors and overcomers.

How Do Believers Get In This Strange Land?

We said this strange land refers to a backslidden state or any kind of state of spiritual decline where the soul is far from God. The Jews in Babylon were carried away captive by their enemies. As a nation they had disobeyed the Lord and were facing God's righteous judgment. We too can be carried away captive, in a spiritual sense. We are carried away captive by the wiles and strategies of Satan. We are carried away by our own lusts and evil hearts. We are carried away by our own emotions and feelings. We must not allow anything or anyone to carry us away captive. We are God's free people!

O for a thousand tongues to sing
My great Redeemer's praise,
The glories of my God and King,
The triumphs of His grace!
My gracious Master and my God,
Assist me to proclaim,
To spread through all the earth abroad
The honors of Thy name.
Jesus! the name that charms our fears,
That bids our sorrows cease;
'Tis music in the sinner's ears,
'Tis life, and health, and peace.
He breaks the power of canceled sin,
He sets the prisoner free;
His blood can make the foulest clean,
His blood availed for me.
Hear Him, ye deaf; His praise, ye dumb,
Your loosened tongues employ;
Ye blind, behold your Savior come,
And leap, ye lame, for joy.

—Charles Wesley

We find ourselves taken captive by the enemy and end up in a strange land for a number reasons. We get into that condition by:

1. Taking our eyes off Christ
2. Forgetting the glory of the gospel
3. Losing sight of our justification and union with Christ
4. Disobedience
5. Rebellion
6. Negligence
7. Being hearers of the Word and not doers of the Word
8. By grieving the Holy Spirit. Ephesians 4:30

Are you in a strange land today? Are you in a state of discouragement, backsliding, defeats, anger, and bitterness, taken captive by ungodly desires or motives that are not honoring to the Lord? This is not the intended life of a true Christian.

How Do Believers Get Out Of This Land?

Deliverance began when they "remembered." Three times in this text of Psalm 137 we find the word "remembered." In verse one we find the word remembered mentioned for the first time in this passage. As the children of Judah had been carried away in the captivity in Babylon, they found themselves camped along the rivers of Babylon. Those that carried them away captive asked these slaves to sing some other songs of worship. It is in this context that these dear people looked back, and in a sense remembered those precious days when they worshipped God in Jerusalem. They remembered the freedom they enjoyed, the wonderful times of fellowship in the temple and in the synagogues. And those memories came haunting back to them as they sat by those muddy rivers of Babylon. Remembering these times brought great sorrow to their hearts. In verse six we find the word remembered for the second time when these people exhorted themselves and said, "If I forget thee, O Jerusalem, let my right hand forget her cunning. If I do not remember thee, let my tongue cleave to the roof of my mouth; if I prefer not Jerusalem above my chief joy." It is in the act of remembering that we are blessed, encouraged, and strengthened to go on in obedience and faith. Finally, in verse 7 they remind the Lord of the Edomites. They said to Jehovah, "Remember O Lord the children of Edom…." The wicked Edomites rejoiced to see the calamities and trials fall on the children of Israel. In seeking help from the Lord they reminded God of the bitter opposition of their enemies. When we are faced with times of temptations, discouragements, loneliness, backsliding, or spiritual pain, look back on those precious times when the Lord met with you. To remember Zion is to remember the Lord. In our case we need to always be ready to look back to our King, the risen Savior, the Lord Jesus Christ. In Romans 2:4 we are exhorted to remember the goodness of God. We should always be ready to remember God's gracious and wonderful promises: Isaiah 41:10, John 14:1-3, Romans 5:1, and Romans 8:1. In the story of the Prodigal Son he came to himself and returned to his father only after he paused long enough to remember those precious times he used to enjoy with his father. When we are facing tough and troubling times, look back and remember God's grace. Gospel themes and truths melt the heart, stir the soul, move us to worship, and open our mouths in continual praise to our God.

The journey home for the children of Israel began with remembering. It would also include repenting of the sins that got them into this trouble in the first place. So it is with each of us as well. We too must repent of our sins and remember how good our God is to each of us if we return to our first love as we are exhorted in Revelation 2:4-5. In this text we read, "Nevertheless, I have this against you, that you have left your first love. Remember therefore from where you have fallen, repent and do the first works...." Remembering and repenting is the way back to God. It is the way to recover our first love to Christ. It is the way to stir our hearts up once again to obedience and praise.

I can summarize the way back to God. Just as the Jews were carried away in the captivity needed to repent, to remember, and returned to the Lord, so too we must repent of our sins, remember the goodness of God, and remember our first love for Jesus Christ. When we repent and remember, our hearts will be stirred within us and we will find strong motivations to return to the Lord. Isn't it interesting that the children of Israel found themselves in a strange land, and those who carried them away captive asked them to sing some of their songs. These dear people said, "How can we sing the Lord's song in a strange land?" Oh I want to tell, you my dear friend, that in my life when I have found myself in a strange land, that is when I found myself in a time of discouragement, despair, loneliness, vicious opposition, and sometimes even in the time of declension, it is usually in times like that I have found that I sing the Lord's song the loudest and the most joyfully.

In April 1948 the Jewish sector of Jerusalem had been cut off during the war for Israeli independence. People were starving and all seemed lost. But a convoy of trucks from Tel Aviv made it through with the much-needed supplies. On one of the trucks someone had painted the words, "If I forget you O Jerusalem...." These words have been both a comfort and a rallying cry for the Jewish people during the times of their persecutions and dispersions.

These people said, "How can we sing the Lord's song in a strange land?" It is precisely here in times of testing, in times of spiritual attack, in times of betrayal that we can sing the Lord's song best.

I Have Walked Alone with Jesus

I've walked alone with Jesus
In a fellowship divine.
Never more can earth allure me,
I am His and He is mine.

On the mountain I have seen Him,
Christ my Comforter and Friend
And the glory of His presence
Will be with me to the end.

I have seen Him, I have known Him,
And He deigns to walk with me;
And the glory of His presence will
be mine eternally.

In the darkness, in the shadows,
With the Savior I have trod

Sweet indeed have been the blessings
Since I walked alone with God.

Oh, the glory of His presence,
Oh, the beauty of His face,
I am His and His forever,
He has saved me by His grace.

—Oswald J. Smith

8
Comfort Ye My People

"Comfort, yes, comfort My people! Says your God." Isaiah 40:1.

"Come now and let us reason together, says the Lord, though your sins are like scarlet, they shall be white as snow; though they are red like Crimson, they shall be as wool." Isaiah 1:18

One of the evidences of being a true Christian is the deep sorrow and guilt we feel when we commit sin. A true Christian who has been born again is deeply ashamed when they fall into sin. Many times they have great doubts about their salvation and question whether they really know the Lord. Some professing Christians can sin very easily and experience very little guilt or shame over it.

If a person can sin without feeling a sense of shame and guilt, this is not a good sign for their soul. Such a person does not need to be comforted but rather needs to be exhorted to examine himself to see if he really is in the faith. But when a true Christian sins, they may take the plunge into deep subjective feelings of sorrow, guilt, and self-doubt. Those who have fallen into sin may need to be comforted by the promises of forgiveness that are found in the word of God. However, I think we should also say that sin in our lives is the great destroyer of inner peace. The Puritan theologian John Owen wisely said, "The vigor and power and comfort of our spiritual life depends on our mortification of the deeds of the flesh."[1]

The mortification of sin is the effort of believers to crucify and put to death the temptations of the flesh. Satan will rob us of our peace if we allow sin to go uncontrolled, unrepented, and unfortified in our lives. Don't allow this thief to steal your joy and your peace from God. Alexander Whyte, an old Scottish theologian from the Free Church of Scotland, made this abundantly clear: "Your peace will be like a river, when you put away your sin; but not one word of true peace, not one drop of true comfort, can you have till then."[2]

Perhaps we should begin by looking at this passage and giving some insights into it as we begin. The word *comfort* comes from a Hebrew word and means "to ease, to console, to give sympathy." The Lord is asking us to bring to His people comfort, sympathy, and to ease their troubled and perplexed hearts and minds.

The phrase "My people," is a beautiful one. What peace and joy it gives us to hear our Lord describe us as, "My people." This text is not given for all people. It is just for His people; for those He has chosen; for those He has regenerated, redeemed, justified, and placed in Christ. This phrase reminds us that we are His treasure, His jewels, His possessions, and His inheritance. How special we are indeed!

- Jeremiah 31:3, "The Lord hath appeared of old unto me, saying, Yea I have loved thee with an everlasting love: therefore with lovingkindness have I drawn thee."

- Ephesians 1:4, "According as he hath chosen us in Him, before the foundation of the world, that we should be holy and without blame before him in love."

I find it especially interesting that the Lord does not say these things in our text to strengthen His people, to make His people successful, to make them self-satisfied, or even to make them self-sufficient. No, the Lord gives us this verse with the express purpose to comfort us. The Lord is writing to His servants. This would include both angels and men. It is by the Holy Spirit that this comfort comes to His people. The Spirit of

God uses both angels and men to comfort the people of God. How do pastors comfort the people of God? Here's a quote from C. H. Spurgeon:

> "Ministers are bound to comfort God's people. I am sure, however, they cannot do it, unless they preach the good old doctrines of truth. Except they preach grace and gracious doctrine, I cannot see how they are to console the Lord's family."[3]

Spurgeon knew the most comforting truth was the precious Gospel of Christ. The Gospel includes all those wonderful and gracious truths that flow from the person and work of Christ.

Why does God give His servants the responsibility to comfort His people? Let me give you several reasons for this request. First, because God loves His people. He is infinitely concerned with their happiness and peace of mind. Second, because despondent Christians bring dishonor and reproach to the cause of Christ. Looking miserable, moaning and groaning, complaining, and murmuring only brings disgrace upon our Lord. Third, because a Christian in a despondent state is distracted and prevented from serving the Lord joyfully, fully, and faithfully. It is difficult to proclaim the good news of the Gospel when our hearts are crushed and broken. Fourth, because we love God's people. The lonely, the crushed, the broken, the hurting, the oppressed, and the bruised are our brothers and sisters. We must be concerned for them or we are not really the Lord's people. One of the tests of a true Christian is to love the brethren.

I would like to give comfort to the people of God in this message. In our text we can pull three precious truths out of this verse. In this verse we are given a gracious invitation from God. Second, we consider the basis of this gracious invitation. And finally, we can consider the promise of this invitation from God.

We Are Given A Gracious Invitation From God

The Lord says to all of His people, and those who have sinned, and to those who feel the weight of their guilt before Him, "Come now, let us reason together…." He is saying, "Let's talk things over." He is saying, "Let's settle matters here and now." The picture here in our text is that something has come between us and our God. So we must take care of it. Even though we have sinned against the Lord, we have this standing invitation to come to the Lord and take care of matters with Him. Most people have no interest in such a meeting. If you desire to come to the presence of God and want to deal with your sins and failures, that is a good sign! God's grace put that desire there in your heart. It is a gracious thing that God so invites us to come into His presence to deal with our sins. How condescending! How amazing! How wonderful that the Almighty invites us to come into His presence to discuss our failures with the promise of forgiving us and wiping our slate clean. This invitation is urgent. "Come now!" The Lord says, "Today if ye will hear his voice, harden not your hearts." Hebrews 3:7 "Behold now is the accepted time, now is the day of salvation." II Corinthians 6:2

The Basis Of This Invitation

The basis of this invitation is the fact that God knows all about our sins and failures. We don't need to minimize our sin. We don't need to paint it, or whitewash it, to make any excuses, or try to make it appear less offensive than it really is. God knows our sins are as scarlet. This refers to the fact that we are stained and blemished in our souls before God.

Although we have sinned and are stained before God, He still invites us to come into His presence. Why does He do so? What motivates our God to invite us, stained as we are and soiled spiritually, to come into His presence? Why would He do such a wonderful thing? There are several reasons for this that we can see from the Scriptures:

- God's electing love, II Thessalonians 2:13, "But we are bound to give thanks always to God for you, brethren beloved of the Lord, because God hath from the beginning chosen you to salvation through sanctification of the Spirit and belief of the truth."

- God's mercy and grace as found in Christ: II Corinthians 8:9, "For ye know the grace of our Lord Jesus Christ, that, though he was rich, yet for your sakes he became poor, that ye through his poverty might be rich."

- God's eternal purpose to mold us and to conform us into the image of His Son Jesus Christ: "For whom he did foreknow, he also did predestinate to be conformed to the image of his Son, that he might be the firstborn among many brethren."

So the basis of this gracious invitation is to be found in these things.

It is based on God's knowledge of our sins and failures, mercy and grace as found in the finished work of His Son, and eternal purpose for our salvation.

The Promise Of This Invitation

The Lord tells us that if we come to Him on His terms and if we settle the issues of our sins, He will clean the stains from our record. "Though your sins be as scarlet, they shall be as white as snow; though they be red like crimson, they shall be as wool." The colors that Isaiah uses in this text are symbolic in nature. The color scarlet is a symbol of the stain of sin on our souls. The Bible makes it clear that we cannot go to Heaven if we do not have a clean and pure record. The color scarlet symbolizes that our record has been soiled and stained before the Lord. The color white, (white as snow and white as wool), symbolizes that when God washes our sins away, He removes the stains, the things that soiled our record and souls. Thus it appears we have a clean record before the Lord. It is like a white page with everything erased that was a mark or blemish on it.

One of the universal problems for all men is to deal with the guilt of our sins and behavior. Guilt is something all men must face and deal with. How do we rid ourselves of true guilt? First, remember there is what we may call false guilt. We must never let people put us on a guilt trip over things the Lord does not say is sin. Second, we must remember not to allow well-meaning sociologists and psychiatrists tell us there is no such thing as guilt. That too would be a great error. We cannot deaden our consciences completely. Sooner or later we must face the facts that we have sinned and have incurred real guilt. At the Nuremberg trials, Nazi collaborator from Poland Hans Frank said with tears in his eyes just before he was to be hanged, "A thousand years will pass and the guilt of Germany will not be erased." He is only partially right. Guilt is never erased until it is washed in the blood of Christ. Only Jesus can wash away the stains on our souls.

The Lord's great concern for His people is to see to it they are given comfort for the trying and difficult times they often face in life. The Lord cries out to His servants, "Comfort ye my people." When we see another believer sad or despondent, we should run to that person and wipe the tears from their eyes.

We should encourage those who feel the weight of their sins and the guilt from them all. This is the first message in this series I intend to give on the subject of giving comfort to God's people. Today I wanted to remind you all that if you have sinned, and if you feel the weight of your sin and guilt, you need not despair. God can wipe away all of your sins and wash them in the precious blood of Christ.

In the Gospel of John we read a very moving and touching story about a woman who was brought before Jesus by the Pharisees and accused of committing adultery. Jesus had been in the Temple teaching. And suddenly this crowd appears and flings this woman down before the Lord's feet. She is trembling, shaking, and ashamed. They boldly announce that she was caught in the very act of adultery. This situation was a setup. They wanted to trap Jesus into making a statement on this issue that would lessen and weaken His appeal to the common people. The religious leaders told Jesus that the law of Moses demands that a woman caught in the act of adultery should be stoned to death. But they wanted to know what He would do with this woman.

Now if Jesus said to do nothing, then the people would conclude that He was soft on sin, and that He was going contrary to the law of Moses. How could He be the Messiah if this were the case? On the other hand, if He says to stone the woman, then the people would conclude that He was a harsh and mean person. They thought they had Jesus between the horns of a dilemma. But our Lord very skillfully navigated through this trap. He stooped down and wrote in the sand. Annoyed by His unwillingness to answer their question, they pressed the issue once again. Jesus finally stood up and addressed these people. He said, "He that is without sin among you let him cast the first stone at this woman." John tells us they began to drop their stones, and one by one they walked away from the woman. Jesus looked down at her and said, "Woman, where are those who accuse you?" And she said, "No one is left to condemn me Lord." So Jesus said to her, "Neither do I condemn you, go and sin no more."

From this story I want you to know that Jesus is concerned about your sins and failures. If you have sinned, listen to His voice speaking to you: "Come now let us reason together saith the Lord, though your sins be as scarlet, they shall be as white as snow, though they be red like crimson, they shall be as wool."

9
Comfort For Those Who Are Discouraged

*P*salm 42:1-11:

To the Chief Musician. A Contemplation of the sons of Korah. As the deer pants for the water brooks, So pants my soul for You, O God. My soul thirsts for God, for the living God. When shall I come and appear before God? My tears have been my food day and night, While they continually say to me, "Where is your God?" When I remember these things, I pour out my soul within me. For I used to go with the multitude; I went with them to the house of God, With the voice of joy and praise, With a multitude that kept a pilgrim feast. Why are you cast down, O my soul? And why are you disquieted within me? Hope in God, for I shall yet praise Him For the help of His countenance. O my God, my soul is cast down within me; Therefore I will remember You from the land of the Jordan, And from the heights of Hermon, From the Hill Mizar. Deep calls unto deep at the noise of Your waterfalls; All Your waves and billows have gone over me. The Lord will command His lovingkindness in the daytime, And in the night His song shall be with me-- A prayer to the God of my life. I will say to God my Rock, "Why have You forgotten me? Why do I go mourning because of the oppression of the enemy?" As with a breaking of my bones, My enemies reproach me, While they say to me all day long, "Where is your God?" Why are you cast down, O my soul? And why are you disquieted within me? Hope in God; For I shall yet praise Him, The help of my countenance and my God.

Isaiah 40:1, reads, "Comfort ye my people." In this text we saw that the infinite and Holy God who created all things instructs His prophets to comfort his people. We said the word *comfort* in this text meant "to ease, to console, to give support and sympathy." The phrase, "My people" was to let us know this is a promise that is only valid for those who are redeemed. A promise is like a coupon that says "valid only at participating stores" or "only valid through such and such a month." How many times have we gone to a store to use a coupon, only to have a clerk say, "This isn't valid," or "isn't good anymore!" So it is with this text. It is only valid or good for the people who know God, those who have:

- Repented of their sins.
- Believed on the Lord Jesus Christ.
- Become His disciples.
- Been dressed in Christ's righteousness and have been washed in His blood.

I want to remind you of how gracious, merciful, and kind our Heavenly Father is with us when we fail and break his commandments. But that is something we have already examined. My goal here is to share with you God's comfort for those who are discouraged. I choose as my text one of David's great Psalms, chapter 42. The title of this Psalm is given in our Bible as "To the chief Musician, Maschil, for the sons of Korah." Eleven Psalms are designated as "to the Maschil" (i.e. as Psalms of instruction.) Here we are taught about the method of finding encouragement from the Lord when we are facing depression or sadness. The sons of Korah were a family of Levitical singers. Korah was the great grandson of Levi. He joined Dathan and Abiram in a terrible rebellion against Moses in the wilderness.

This particular Psalm was written when David was running from his own son, Absalom. This took place when that terrible civil war broke out and Absalom used a military coup to seize power from his father. As David is on the run, he can no longer come to the Tabernacle in Jerusalem to worship the Lord. In David's lonely exile, he longs to worship God in the Tabernacle. It is while under these deep feelings of sadness and rejection that David writes this Psalm.

My theme for this message is "Comfort For Those Who Are Discouraged." There are three points that we need to consider in this text:

- The definition of David's discouragement
- The description of David's discouragement
- The deliverance of David from his discouragement.

The Definition Of David's Discouragement

First, let's consider the definition of David's discouragement. In this particular Psalm, David is discouraged specifically because he was banished and exiled by his own countrymen. David was also betrayed by his own son, Absalom, who was bitter because David did not punish Absalom's half brother for the rape of his sister, Tamar. David is brokenhearted over the sins and the sufferings of his people that this terrible civil war brought upon them. Because of all this, David cannot worship in the Tabernacle in Jerusalem. These were the reasons David was so deeply discouraged.

But how about us today? There are many reasons why we become discouraged today. Here are just a few of the reasons that may cause us to become discouraged.

First, we are sometimes discouraged because of our disobedience. Committing sin can cause us to lose our peace with God, and we become discouraged.

Second, we can become discouraged because of disappointments in our lives. How many times do we hear people say, "We thought," "we had hoped," "we wanted," "we desired," etc.? Disappointments can lead us into the valley of despair.

Third, we can become discouraged because of disillusionments. Our disappointments lead to despair. Our dreams don't materialize and we sink beneath the waves of sorrow. This feeling of disillusionment has been one of the many experiences of the people of God through the centuries. Maxwell Cornelious wrote this wonderful hymn:

> "Not now but in the coming years,
> It may be in the better land,
> We'll read the meaning of our tears,
> And then sometime we'll understand.
>
> We'll catch the broken thread again,
> And finish what we here began.
> Heaven will the mysteries explain,
> And then, ah then, we'll understand,

We'll know why clouds instead of sun,
Were over many a cherished plan.
Why song has ceased when scarce begun,
Tis there, up there we'll understand.

Why what we long for most of all,
Eludes so oft our eager hands,
Why hopes are crushed, and castles fall,
Up there sometime we'll understand.

God knows the way He holds the key.
He guides with unerring hand,
Sometime with tearless eyes we'll see.
Yes there, up there, we'll understand.

Fourth, disease is another reason we may find ourselves discouraged and depressed. Diseases and sicknesses can wreak havoc on our bodies, our minds, sap our strength, and eventually wear us out spiritually.

Fifth, distractions are another way we often find ourselves depressed. The cares and worries of life can distract us from doing the things that matter most in our relationship with the Lord. We need to be very careful lest we become distracted and find ourselves neglecting to replenish the wells of our salvation.

In spite of the many reasons we may fall into periods of discouragement, the Bible exhorts us to avoid this spirit of discouragement.

The Lord tells us in Joshua 1:9, "Have I not commanded you? Be strong, and of good courage; do not be afraid, nor be dismayed, for the Lord your God is with you wherever you go."

Peter tells his readers, "Casting all your care upon Him, for. He cares for you." I Peter 5:7.

Isaiah tells us:

"But those who wait on the Lord shall renew their strength; They shall mount up with wings like eagles, they shall run and not be weary, they shall walk and not faint." Isaiah 40:31

The Description Of David's Discouragement

Let's consider the description of David's depression. In this particular Psalm, David uses a number of adjectives and analogies to describe the discouragement that he faces. In vs. 1, he uses the analogy of a deer panting (lit. looking for, longing for, sighing for, etc.) after the water brooks while chased by the hounds or wolves. In vs. 2, he describes his discouragement as a deep spiritual thirst for the living God. In vs. 3, he says his "tears" (weeping have been his "meat," i.e., food). Instead of eating he wept. Often discouragements take away our appetite and cause us to fast. In vs. 4, he says his discouragement caused him to "pour out his soul." David is melting and collapsing; he is just becoming like a flow of water. His sorrows just gush and flow out of his heart. In vs. 5, 6, 11, he describes himself as being "cast down," (i.e. bowed down, dejected, sad, etc.) In vs. 7, he says, "all thy waves and billows are gone over me." These are the terrible discouragements David faced. What did he do with them? How did David handle these things, and how did he view them personally?

First, David recognizes his troubles and sorrows are from the Lord! See Romans 8:28: "And we know that all things work together for good..." and I Thessalonians 5:18, "In everything give thanks; for this is the will of God in Christ Jesus for you." Secondly, David sees himself being overwhelmed by waves or floods of depression, loneliness, doubts, and griefs. David is being drowned in his griefs. There is something so simple but so sublime in the old Negro spiritual, "Nobody knows the sorrows I've been through, nobody knows but Jesus." In vs. 9, David says his discouragements are like the feelings of being forsaken and forgotten by God. See Isaiah 49:13-16:

> "Sing, O heavens! Be joyful, O earth! And break out in singing, O mountains! For the Lord has comforted His people, And will have mercy on His afflicted. But Zion said, "The Lord has forsaken me, And my Lord has forgotten me." "Can

a woman forget her nursing child, And not have compassion on the son of her womb? Surely they may forget, Yet I will not forget you. See, I have inscribed you on the palms of My hands; Your walls are continually before Me."

In vs. 9, David says, "I go mourning…" In vs. 10, David compares his discouragements to "a sword in my bones." In other words, it is very painful, it hurts, and it cuts to his very soul.

This discouragement is very real. If you've never been there, it might be hard for you to comprehend David's description. Sorrow and discouragement like this needs the mercy and grace of God.

The Way David Was Delivered From His Discouragement

First, let me say that sometimes this kind of sorrow may last a long time. We often pass through a season of discouragement. "Weeping may endure for a night but joy cometh in the mourning." Second, let me say that we need to be very patient and understanding with those in these kinds of valleys, pits, and dark nights of the soul.

Here are the steps David took to bring relief to his soul:

- He put his hope in God, vs. 5. God has not changed. Hebrews 13:8, "Jesus Christ is the same yesterday, today, and forever."

- He remembered God's past dealings with him, vs.6. Psalm 40:1-3, "To the Chief Musician. A Psalm of David. I waited patiently for the Lord; And He inclined to me, And heard my cry. He also brought me up out of a horrible pit, Out of the miry clay, And set my feet upon a rock, And established my steps. He has put a new song in my mouth-- Praise to our God; Many will see it and fear, And will trust in the Lord." Romans 2:4, "Or do you despise the riches of His goodness, forbearance, and longsuffering, not knowing that the goodness of God leads you to repentance?"

- He remembered God's promises, vs.8. Isaiah 41:10, "Fear not, for I am with you; Be not dismayed, for I am your God. I will strengthen you, Yes, I will help you, I will uphold you with My righteous right hand." Isaiah 49:13-16, "Sing, O heavens! Be joyful, O earth! And break out in singing, O mountains! For the Lord has comforted His people, And will have mercy on His afflicted. But Zion said, "The Lord has forsaken me, And my Lord has forgotten me." "Can a woman forget her nursing child, And not have compassion on the son of her womb? Surely they may forget, Yet I will not forget you. See, I have inscribed you on the palms of My hands; Your walls are continually before Me." Ephesians 1:6, "to the praise of the glory of His grace, by which He made us accepted in the Beloved."

- He spoke to God and remembered He has a purpose for us in our times of trial. Job 23:10, "But He knows the way that I take; When He has tested me, I shall come forth as gold." Romans 5:3, "And not only that, but we also glory in tribulations, knowing that tribulation produces perseverance;" Philippians 1:2, "Grace to you and peace from God our Father and the Lord Jesus Christ." Hebrews 12:5-8, "And you have forgotten the exhortation which speaks to you as to sons: "My son, do not despise the chastening of the Lord, Nor be discouraged when you are rebuked by Him; For whom the Lord loves He chastens, And scourges every son whom He receives." If you endure chastening, God deals with you as with sons; for what son is there whom a father does not chasten? But if you are without chastening, of which all have become partakers, then you are illegitimate and not sons." James 1:2-3, "My brethren, count it all joy when you fall into various trials, knowing that the testing of your faith produces patience."

- He remembered he was not alone in his sufferings, vs.4. Phil. 3:10, "that I may know Him, and the power of his resurrection, and the fellowship of his sufferings." Hebrews 12: 3, "For consider him that endured such contradiction of sinners against himself, lest ye be wearied and faint in your minds."

- He submitted to God's sovereignty, vs.7. He refers to these trials as "Thy waves," and "Thy billows." God is too wise to err, and too loving to be unkind.

If we are faithful to the commands of our God, we should work hard at giving comfort to God's people in their times of discouragement. This, after all, is what we are commanded to do in Isaiah 40.

My dear friends, if you are discouraged, let it be remembered that Jesus understands your feelings. He sees your tears. Jesus Himself was described as, "A man of sorrows, and acquainted with grief." Look at Him with your mind's eye; see Him:

- Weeping over Jerusalem.
- Weeping and grieving with Mary and Martha at the death of Lazarus.

- Being overwhelmed with sorrow and grief at Gethsemane.
- Crying out on the Cross, "My God, My God, why hast Thou forsaken Me?"

Ah, yes, Jesus understands you! "Jesus loves me this I know, for the Bible tells me so!" I close here with the words of the great hymn by Horatio Spafford:

When peace like a river attendeth my way,
When sorrows like sea billows roll.
What ever my lot, Thou hast taught me to say,
It is well, it is well, with my soul.

Though Satan should buffet, and trials should come,
Let this bless assurance control.
For Christ has regarded my helpless estate,
And hath shed His own blood for my soul

My sin, ah the bliss, of this glorious thought,
My sin not in part, but the whole.
Is nailed to His Cross, and I bear it no more.
Praise the Lord, Praise the Lord, oh l my soul!

We considered the steps David took to overcome his discouragement. These steps are very important and should be implemented when we find ourselves wallowing in the "Slough Of Despond." Another look at the way to overcome discouragement may be of some help.

The word *discouragement* comes from the root word *courage*. The prefix *dis-* means "the opposite of." So discouragement is the opposite of courage. When we are discouraged, we have lost the motivation to press forward. The mountain seems too steep, the valley too dark, or the battle too fierce, and we lose the courage to continue.

In many places throughout Scripture, God commands His people to take courage (Psalm 27:14; 31:24; 2 Chronicles 32:7; Deuteronomy 31:6). When God selected Joshua to replace Moses as the leader of the Israelites, some of His first words to Joshua were "Have I not commanded you? Be strong and courageous. Do not be afraid; do not be discouraged, for the LORD your God will be with you wherever you go" (Joshua 1:9). The Lord based this command upon His previous promise to Joshua in verse 6: "As I was with Moses, so I will be with you; I will never leave you nor forsake you." The Lord knew Joshua was going to face some big battles, and He did not want His servant to become discouraged.

The key to overcoming discouragement is to remember God's promises and apply them. When we know the Lord, we can stand upon the promises He has given His people in His Word. Whether or not we see the fulfillment of those promises in this life, His promises still stand (Hebrews 11:13–16). This knowledge kept the apostle Paul pressing forward, preaching the gospel, eventually ending up in a Roman jail where he lost his life. From prison, he wrote, "I press on toward the goal for the prize of the upward call of God in Christ Jesus" (Philippians 3:14). He could press on through persecution, rejection, beatings, and discouragement because his eyes were on the ultimate prize: hearing the words "Well done!" from his Lord and Savior (see Matthew 25:23; Revelation 22:12)."[1]

Just as the Lord was with the three Hebrew boys who were tossed into the fiery furnace of the King of Babylon, so too the Lord will be with each of us when we pass through the fires of persecution and tribulation. When we suffer, we never suffer alone. David was keenly aware that even in his banishment and exile as he was running from his rebellious son, Absalom, the Lord was with him. Sometimes I think I can handle anything if I know the Lord is with me and approves of my life. In the end, in every situation, the presence of God makes everything right. Amen!

By Robert L. Dickie

10
Comfort For Those Who Are Dying

Psalm 116:15, "Precious in the sight of the Lord is the death of His saints."

Using Psalm 116:15 as my text, I want to give comfort for those who are near death, and to all of us who will one day take our flight to the other side of the veil to meet the Lord. As much as we should each be excited to meet the Lord, it is in our very nature to resist the approach of death. We have never walked down that path before and it brings us to the end of our earthy pilgrimage. So it is natural to tremble at the approach of this great enemy. It is a joy when we are reminded that our Lord and Savior conquered sin, death, and hell on our behalf. We may tremble at the approach of death, but never forget the Lord you serve came out of the tomb and He lives as the risen and glorified Son of God.

This Psalm of worship was written by David to celebrate his deliverance from various perils and trials. In the midst of these verses David makes a statement that has been a comfort to Christians through the centuries. He writes in verse 15, "Precious in the sight of the Lord is the death of His saints." This word *precious* is a Hebrew word that means "honorable, glorious, dear, and rare." It is a natural feeling to recoil at the thought and the approach of death. How can we find anything about this subject that could possibly be good, let alone precious? David, in this text, tells us how to find comfort in this mysterious subject.

When people are nearing death, it is a great comfort for them to know how precious in the sight of the Lord the death of His saints really is. I want to answer three questions concerning this topic.

- Who Are The Saints Of God?
- Why Is Death Precious To God's Saints?
- How Does One Become A Saint?

By Robert L. Dickie

Who Are The Saints Of God?

The Hebrew word for *saint* is *chasid* and means "kind and pious one." Sometimes the Hebrew word was *gadosh* meaning "holy one." The Roman Catholic Church has officially recognized some people and has canonized them (i.e. has made or declared them to be saints). In the view of Rome, only a certain few people ever reach sainthood. But the biblical idea is that all who have been born again, who have been washed in the blood of Jesus and have been clothed in His righteousness are saints (i.e. His holy ones, pious one, etc.).

The evidences of being a saint are clearly marked in Scripture:

- Saints are holy, John 14:15, "If ye love me keep my commandments."

- Saints are those who follow Christ, John 10:27, "My sheep hear my voice, and I know them, and they follow me."

- Saints are those who worship God in Spirit and in Truth, John 4:24, "God is a Spirit: and they that worship him must worship him in spirit and in truth."

- Saints are those people who love the brethren, John 13:34-35, "A new commandment I give unto you, That ye love one another; as I have loved you, that ye also love one another. By this shall all men know that ye are my disciples, if ye have love one to another."

- Saints are those people who have come to Christ, John 6:37, "All that the Father giveth me shall come to me, and he that cometh to Me I will in no wise cast out."

Now, in our text, David does not say death is precious for all people, he limits his words to the saints of God. If the Roman Catholic view of sainthood were true, this verse would be of no comfort to the ordinary person when it came time to die. Likewise, for all those who live their lives apart from the Church, who live in rebellion to God, who refuse to come to Christ, must not take comfort in this verse. Death is not precious for everyone.

Why Is Death Precious To God's Saints?

Death in general and in itself is not a good thing. In death the noblest work of God is unraveled and undone. The skillful embroidery of the human body is destroyed. Consider with me the estimate that Jesus and the Apostle Paul put on death. In John 17:24, Jesus said, "Father, I will that they also, whom thou hast given me, be with me where I am; that they may behold my glory, which thou hast given me before the foundation of the world." Jesus prayed that all those the Father had given Him would eventually be brought to Him in glory. So at death, while we are grieving the loss of our loved ones here, Jesus and those in heaven are rejoicing over there. We have a hard time letting go of those we love who must leave our world. And yet for those who die in Christ, they set off for a far better place. This reminds me of the reading on death that I have often read. It is entitled:

Life Everlasting

I am standing upon the seashore; a ship at my side spreads her white sails to the morning breeze and starts for the blue ocean.

She is an object of beauty and strength, and I stand and watch her until at length she hangs like a speck of white cloud just where the sea and the sky come down to mingle with each other. Then someone at my side says, "There! She's gone!"

Gone where? Gone from my sight—that's all. She is just as large in mast and hull and spar as she was when she left my side and just as able to bear her load of living freight to the place of destination.

Her diminished size is in me, not in her; and just at the moment when someone at my side says, "There! She's gone."—There are other eyes watching her coming and other voices ready to take up the glad shout, "There she comes!"…and that is dying.

Paul writes to the Philippians in chapter 4, verses 13-18, and says:

> "For I am in a strait betwixt two, having a desire to depart, and to be with Christ; which is far better: Nevertheless to abide in the flesh is more needful for you." And to the Thessalonians he writes, "But I would not have you to be ignorant, brethren, concerning them which are asleep, that ye sorrow not, even as others which have no hope. For if we believe that Jesus died and rose again, even so them also which sleep in Jesus will God bring with him For this we say unto you by the word of the Lord, that we which are alive and remain unto the coming of the Lord shall not prevent them which are asleep. For the Lord himself shall descend from heaven with a shout, with the voice of the archangel, and with the trump of God: and the dead in Christ shall rise first: Then we which are alive and remain shall be caught up together with them in the clouds, to meet the Lord in the air: and so shall we ever be with the Lord. Wherefore comfort one another with these words."

It is clear from Paul's words that he had a high view of death and Heaven. Paul understood that death would bring him into the presence of Christ, and, for this reason, he longed to go to Heaven to be with Him. However, for the unredeemed, death only brings grief and fear:

- Death brings separation.
- Death brings an end of their hopes and dreams.
- Death brings sorrow and pain.
- Death brings fear of the future and uncertainty of what to expect beyond the grave.
- Death brings the judgment of God.

In contrast to the unbeliever, what does death bring to the believer who is the saint of God? Whatever it is it must be wonderful because Psalm 116:15 tells us, "Precious in the sight of the Lord is the death of His saints."

There are six reasons I want to share with you to explain why death is precious to the believer.

First, death brings an end to earthly trials and sorrows, Revelation 21:4, "And God shall wipe away all tears from their eyes; and there shall be no more death, neither sorrow, nor crying, neither shall there be any more pain: for the former things are passed away."

Second, death brings us to our eternal reward. We see this truth illustrated in the parable of the talents, Mathew 25:14-30:

"For the kingdom of heaven is as a man traveling into a far country, who called his own servants, and delivered unto them his goods. And unto one he gave five talents, to another two, and to another one; to every man according to his several ability; and straightway took his journey. Then he that had received the five talents went and traded with the same, and made them other five talents. And likewise he that had received two, he also gained other two. But he that had received one went and digged in the earth, and hid his lord's money. After a long time the Lord of those servants cometh, and reckoneth with them. And so he that had received five talents came and brought other five talents, saying, Lord, thou deliveredst unto me five talents: behold, I have gained beside them five talents more. His Lord said unto him, Well done, thou good and faithful servant: thou hast been faithful over a few things, I will make thee ruler over many things: enter thou into the joy of thy Lord. He also that had received two talents came and said, Lord, thou deliveredst unto me two talents: behold, I have gained two other talents beside them. His Lord said unto him, Well done, good and faithful servant; thou hast been faithful over a few things, I will make thee ruler over many things: enter thou into the joy of thy Lord. Then he which had received the one talent came and said, Lord, I knew thee that thou art an hard man, reaping where thou hast not sown, and gathering where thou hast not strawed: And I was afraid, and went and hid thy talent in the earth: lo, there thou hast that is thine. His Lord answered and said unto him, Thou wicked and slothful servant, thou knewest that I reap where I sowed not, and gather where I have not strawed: Thou oughtest therefore to have put my money to the exchangers, and then at my coming I should have received mine own with usury. Take therefore the talent from him, and give it unto him which hath ten talents. For unto every one that hath shall be given, and he shall have abundance: but from him that hath not shall be taken away even that which he hath. And cast ye the unprofitable servant into outer darkness: there shall be weeping and gnashing of teeth.

The parable of the talents reminds us that in the life to come there will be rewards; there will be future service based on our faithfulness and obedience to the light we had here on earth. "To whom much is given much shall be required." Luke 12:48

Third, death brings us to a place of eternal rest. The battle against:

- Indwelling sin is over.
- The world, the flesh, and the devil is over.
- Death, disease, and decay is over.

When that old Puritan Richard Baxter was dying, a friend asked him, "Dear Mr. Baxter, how are you?" and he replied, "Almost well!" Death for the believer is the ultimate cure and healing for all our sorrows and needs.

Fourth, death brings us into fellowship with the Church Triumphant. The saints walk with:

- Patriarchs
- Apostles
- Church Fathers
- Reformers
- The holy men and women of all the ages

Fifth, death brings us into the immediate and manifest presence of God the Father. This is what thrills the soul of those who die in Christ. The great missionary to the Native American Indians said on his death bed:

"I am almost in eternity. I long to be there. My work is done. I have done with all my friends. All the world is now nothing to me. Oh, to be in heaven, to praise and glorify God with his holy angels."[1]

Sixth, death brings us into the intimate and immediate presence of God's dear Son Jesus Christ. "To be absent from the body is to be present with the Lord." II Corinthians 5:8

We should notice that our text says, "Precious in the sight of the Lord is the death of His saints." God sees us at all times. God is watching over us. Nothing happens to us by chance or by accident. Our days are ordained by a sovereign providence. Whether we are delivered from death, or whether we are called home to the Lord, it does not matter. God sees and is most concerned about us. He is not an absentee landlord or caretaker who doesn't care.

How Does One Become A Saint?

From the divine perspective:

- God chooses a people.
- God regenerates a people.
- God redeems a people.
- God justifies a people.
- From beginning to end, it is all by the grace of God.

From the human perspective:

- We must repent of our sins.
- We must receive Jesus Christ as our Lord and Savior.
- We must follow Christ daily in obedience.
- All three of these things must be true of us.

If we are dying, or if we come to that time and place in our lives when death is going to claim us and number us among its victims, then this text from the pen of David is a great comfort to us. Consider with me what some of the great saints have said when they faced death and knew their time on this earth was about to be finished:

- Harrington Evans, "Tell my people that I am accepted in the beloved."

- John Rees, "Christ in the glory of His person, Christ in the love of His heart, Christ in the power of His arm, this is the rock I stand on, and now death strikes!"

- When the great scientist Michael Faraday was dying a journalist asked him about his speculations for a life after death. "Speculations!" he said, "I know nothing about speculations. I'm resting on certainties. I know that my Redeemer liveth, and because He lives, I shall live also."

- David Brainard, "I do not go to heaven to be advanced," he said to Jonathan Edwards on his death bed. "I go to heaven to give honor to God. It is no matter where I shall be stationed in heaven, whether I have a high or low seat there, but to live and please and glorify God... My heaven is to please God and to glorify Him, and to give Him all the glory, and to be devoted to his service."

- D.L. Moody, a few hours before he died caught a glimpse of the glory awaiting him. Awakening from sleep, he said, "Earth recedes, Heaven opens before me. If this is death, it is sweet! There is no valley here. God is calling me, and I must go."

His son, who was standing by his bedside said, "Father, you must be dreaming."

"No, I am not dreaming: I have been within the gates; I have seen the children's faces."

A short time elapsed and then, following what seemed to the family to be the death struggle, he spoke again: "This is my triumph; this my coronation day! It is glorious."

- John Wesley said, "Our people die well." Asked why that was so, he replied, "Because they spent their lives preparing for their departure."

How do we prepare for death? How do we get ready for our departure? Let me first present the negative side, and explain the wrong way to prepare for death. To prepare for death we must not be focused mainly on keeping rules and regulations. We must not be focused on separating from worldliness. We must not be focused on priding ourselves on the things we either do or don't do. These kinds of things have a tendency to promote pride and self-righteousness. It creates the attitude that I'm ready for Heaven because I'm so good, I'm so obedient, or because I've done better than others. If we prepare for death by focusing on all the things we've done, then we are really no better than the Pharisees. On the positive side, here is how we are to prepare for death. We must work out our salvation with fear and trembling. Philippians 2:13. This means we must work through the great biblical doctrines we find taught in Paul's Epistles. We need to examine ourselves in the light of the Scriptures and ask such relevant and penetrating questions as these:

- Have we been regenerated? Are we born again? Has the life of God been planted in our souls? Pharisees were great at rules and regulations but were missing the divine life of God in their souls. They strained at gnats and swallowed camels. Have we been justified by faith? Are we covered in Christ's righteousness? Do we realize the only way we can approach a holy God is not on the basis of our obedience, but on the basis of Christ's obedience? Do we realize this? Is our hope grounded on this alone?

- Have we made our calling and election sure? Have we considered our lives to see if we have the fruits of grace, the evidence of salvation?

- Are we growing in grace? Do we hunger and thirst for righteousness?

- Do we love and appreciate the things of God?

- Do we repent of our sins? Here is where our obedience is important. Keeping God's laws, obeying principles, separating from sin is not the *basis* of our acceptance with God. These things should be a *result* of our acceptance with God.

Do you see the difference I am making here? The legalist, the moralist, the Pharisee keeps laws, commandments, and regulations as the basis of their hope of Heaven. They pride themselves on all they have done. But the believer keeps God's laws and commandments as a result of his hope of Heaven. They keep the commandments of the Lord because they love Him. They are not filled with pride, but with deep humility. Their focus is not on how good they've been, but on how gracious God has been.

To summarize, the way to prepare for death and Heaven, we should focus on these four things:

1. We should work out our salvation with fear and trembling.

2. We should feast on Christ continually.

3. We should live out the Gospel and never tire of the Gospel.

4. We should examine ourselves in the light of God's Word, and work through the great doctrines of the faith such as Regeneration, Calling, Justification, Election, Sanctification, and Glorification.

One way of preparing for death is to pray the prayers found in the Bible that others used to call on God at the time of their death:

- "To you, O LORD, I lift up my soul." Psalm 25:1

- "Though I should walk in the valley of the shadow of death, no evil would I fear, for You are with me." Psalm 23:4

- "Into Your hands I commend My spirit." Luke 23:46

- "Jesus, remember me when you come into your kingdom." Luke 23:42

- "Lord Jesus, receive my spirit." Acts 7:59

Fanny Crosby had written a special poem she called her "Soul's poem." It was almost too intimate for her to share with anyone. It was based on a few verses from Ecclesiastes 12:6 and Revelation 22:4-5. For years she never shared it with anyone. Professor Kenneth Osbeck says its revelation to the public came about this way. One day at a Bible conference in Northfield Massachusetts, Miss Crosby was asked by D. L. Moody to give a personal testimony concerning her faith and Christian experience. At first she hesitated, then quietly rose and said: "There is one hymn which I have written that has never been published. I call it my 'Soul's poem.' Sometimes when I am troubled, I repeat it to myself, for it brings comfort to my heart." She then recited it while many were blessed, and some even wept. This poem has now been published and it conveys Fanny Crosby's thoughts of death and Heaven.

Saved By Grace

Someday the silver cord will break,
And I no more as now shall sing,
But oh, the joy when I shall wake
Within the palace of the King!

Someday my earthly house will fall,
I cannot tell how soon twill be;
But this I know my All in All
Has now a place in Heaven for me.

Someday, when fades the golden sun
Beneath the rosy tinted west,
My blessed Lord will say, "Well Done!"
And I shall enter into rest.

Someday: till then I'll watch and wait,
My lamp all trimmed and burning bright,
That when my Saviour opes the gate,
My soul to Him may take its flight.

And I shall see Him face to face,
And tell the story saved by grace;
And I shall see Him face to face,
And tell the story saved by grace.

Psalm 116:15 tells us, "Precious in the sight of the Lord is the death of His saints." How wonderful is this great promise! May we all find peace and comfort from this text today.

11
Comfort For Those Who Are Lonely

Proverbs 18:24, "A man who has friends must himself be friendly, But there is a friend who sticks closer than a brother."

*I*n this series on comfort we have considered the following topics: comfort for those who have been tempted, comfort for those who have sinned, comfort for those who are discouraged, comfort for those who are dying or near death. Now we will consider comfort for those who are lonely.

It may seem strange that we speak of those who may be lonely. We might say, "How can a person be lonely in the Church of Jesus Christ?" As strange as it may seem, there are many in our churches who are indeed lonely. Even the Lord Jesus Himself was lonely at various times during His earthly ministry. One such time was during His agony in the garden of Gethsemane. In Matthew's Gospel chapter 26 verse 36-39, we read:

> "Then cometh Jesus with them unto a place called Gethsemane, and saith unto the disciples, Sit ye here, while I go and pray yonder. And he took with him Peter and the two sons of Zebedee, and began to be sorrowful and very heavy. Then saith he unto them, My soul is exceeding sorrowful, even unto death: tarry ye here, and watch with me. And he went a little farther, and fell on his face, and prayed, saying, O my Father, if it be possible, let this cup pass from me: nevertheless not as I will, but as thou wilt."

We see in this text that Jesus began to be very sorrowful and very heavy hearted. He said to His disciples that He was "exceeding sorrowful." The idea here is that Jesus was feeling a longing for Heaven, for the fellowship with His Father, for the comfort of the communion of the Trinity. Jesus, as the God Man, was basically lonely and homesick at this point. How do we account for these feelings in our Savior? Jesus sees the hour approaching of His death and passion. But along with that, He sees His disciples are deserting Him and He is becoming more and more isolated. As this takes place, Jesus finds Himself being overwhelmed by wave upon wave of sorrow. Loneliness results from such feelings of isolation. If our Savior knew such times as these, we must not be surprised if we from time to time experience the same feelings.

Perhaps at this point we should give a basic definition of what it means to be lonely:

> "Loneliness is, therefore, a state of mind, an emotion brought on by feelings of separation from other human beings. The sense of isolation is very deeply felt by those who are lonely. The Hebrew word translated *desolate* or *lonely* in the Old Testament means 'one alone, only; one who is solitary, forsaken, wretched.' There is no deeper sadness that ever comes over the mind than the idea that we are alone in the world, that we do not have a friend, that no one cares for us, that no one is concerned about anything that might happen to us, that no one would care if we were to die or shed a tear over our grave."[1]

Notice the main things he identifies as the root of being lonely:

1. A desire to be connected.
2. A desire to hear from someone.
3. A desire to be affirmed, to be considered important to someone.
4. A desire to be remembered at special times.

Loneliness can be a great weight and burden to all kinds of people. A college student away from home for the first time may know times of loneliness. They feel this weight grow with each passing day they do not hear from home or from their friends. Parents may feel a sense of loneliness when their children have moved away from home and do not call, write, or visit. Wives may feel lonely in a marriage when their husbands do not share or communicate clearly and frequently. Many older people in nursing homes face the pain of loneliness when no one comes to visit them on a regular basis. Life can be full of deep pains and wrenching sorrows when we feel disconnected and isolated from those we love and desire to hear from. There are two points I want us to consider on this subject: the Bible's solution for loneliness and the Lord Jesus as the ultimate solution for loneliness.

The Bible's Solution For Loneliness

There are many problems we face in life. The proper remedy for problems such as grief, disappointments, heartache, suffering, sorrow, temptation, and loneliness, are found in the promises of God's Word. We are looking at loneliness specifically. Now when it comes to loneliness, the Bible offers a number of solutions.

First there is the solution of fellowship. This is Christian koinonia. This is the meeting of one another's needs through the joys and intimate relationships that are formed in the local church. Christian fellowship involves sharing, caring, ministry, and fellowshipping around the Word of God and His Son Jesus Christ.

Second, there is the solution of friendship. Christian friendship is described in Proverbs 17:17, "A friend loveth at all times, and a brother is born for adversity." Christian friendship involves having friends being with us at all times, even when things are going badly. Beware of fair-weather friends who gather like vultures around the successful and prosperous, but who disappear when fortunes fade or turn south. Christian friendship is also described by the verb *love*. What is love? Love is:

1. Patient
2. Kind
3. Not envious
4. Bears all things
5. Thinketh no evil
6. Endures all things
7. Forbears with others
8. Turns the other cheek
9. Goes the extra mile
10. Never fails
11. Turns a blind eye and has a deaf ear

Someone has said that to have one true friend is to be rich. Indeed, the importance of having good Christian friends is seen in the life of the Apostle Paul. His list of special Christian friends would have included Aquila and Priscila with whom he occasionally worked and lived (see Acts 18:3); Onesiphorous "for he oft refreshed me." II Timothy 1:16, and Philemon, whom he writes about: "For we have great joy and consolation in thy love, because the hearts of the saints are refreshed by thee, brother." Luke was a special Christian friend and a host of others. God "comforted us," he wrote when describing the weariness of his own soul, "by the coming of Titus" II Corinthians 7:6. On a terribly tiring trip to Rome, there was a moment when the brethren from the church heard that Paul was not far from his destination and came to meet him: "And from thence, when the brethren heard of us, they came to meet us as far as Appiiforum and The three taverns: whom when Paul saw, he thanked God, and took courage." From these passages we see that Paul's friends, comforted him, refreshed him, encouraged him, cared for him, helped him, prayed for him, and met many of his physical and financial needs.

Third, there is the solution of a loyal and loving partner. In Genesis we read, "And the Lord God said, It is not good that the man should be alone; I will make him an help meet for him." One of the Bible's solutions for loneliness is God's design for marriage. But not everyone is married, and some people find themselves in a relationship where they may have an unsaved partner who does not measure up to the biblical standards and ideals for marriage, or they may have a Christian partner who is failing at this very point.

These are the solutions the Bible holds out for us. To summarize, they are:

1. Fellowship
2. Friendship
3. Marriage or partnership

It is important that believers who are lonely seek to develop these kinds of ties in the Church and in their homes. But what do we do when, for whatever reason, we have difficulty with these three areas in our lives? The Bible and our Lord does not leave us without a second and more powerful resource to help us.

The Lord Jesus Is The Ultimate Solution For Our Loneliness

Whether or not we can find true and meaningful fellowship in the Church, we should find in Christ a deep and satisfying fellowship. John tells us in I John 1:3, "That which we have seen and heard declare we unto you, that ye also may have fellowship with us: and truly our fellowship is with the Father, and with His Son Jesus Christ."

There should never be in a believer's life a sense of disconnection. We have the preciousness of our relationship with the Lord Jesus Christ. The dynamic fellowship with Christ should be overwhelming to our hearts. Even in our Christian hymns we sing of this: "What a fellowship, what a joy divine, leaning on the everlasting arms..." The great German martyr Dietrich Bonhoeffer writes about the powerful influence of Christian fellowship on the Church. He says:

> "A Christian fellowship lives and exists by the intercession of its members for one another...I can no longer condemn or hate a brother for whom I pray, no matter how much trouble he causes me. His face, hitherto may have been strange and intolerable to me, is transformed in intercession into the countenance of a brother for whom Christ died, the face of a forgiven sinner. This is the happy discovery for the Christian who begins to pray for others. There is no dislike, no personal tension, no estrangement that cannot be overcome by intercession as far as our side of it is concerned..."

When we gather for fellowship, we should find ourselves praying for one another, sharing and caring for one another, and encouraging one another.

Again, whether we find friendship in the Church,

we should find it in the Lord Jesus Christ. Jesus taught His disciples that He was now the friend of sinners. In John 15:14, He says, "Ye are my friends, if ye do whatsoever I command you." Proverbs 18:24 reads, "…There is a friend that sticketh closer than a brother." A brother is one who has a natural inclination to stay close to a blood brother. But Jesus is One who is even more faithful, loyal, and true than our natural brothers. David and Jonathan in the book of 1 Samuel give us a picture of Jesus whose love for us is greater than that of a brother. David says, "I am distressed for thee, my brother Jonathan: very pleasant hast thou been unto me: thy love to me was wonderful, passing the love of women." The love between David and Jonathan was not a sexual love. It was the love of two kindred spirits that united them in a deep and intimate friendship. They were one in their goals, purposes, and desires.

I love the old hymn, "What a friend we have in Jesus, all our sins and griefs to bear…" this hymn was written by a man named Joseph Scriven. Joseph was an Irish immigrant. He was deeply in love with his fiancé and were planning to be married. Just before their marriage she drowned in a tragic accident. Joseph Scriven became embittered and angry at God. He could find no peace or comfort. Eventually a friend led him to Christ and a great peace flooded his soul. It was then he was able to write the words to this great Christian hymn, "What A Friend We Have In Jesus."

Finally, we should find in our marriages that blessing of love and companionship that our wives and husbands should provide. But even there, if we are unmarried, or do not have the kind of partners who are filling the empty void in our lonely hearts, Jesus is our husband, and we are His bride. Paul writes, "Husbands love your wives even as Christ loved the Church, and gave himself for her." What can a friend, or a person we fellowship with, and our partner in marriage do for us? They can calm the storm of our lives, fill the emptiness, help encourage us when we are down or lonely, and meet the intimate needs of our souls. It has been said that "Sometimes the Lord calms the storm; sometimes He lets the storm rage and calms the child." Even in the absence of a friend, or one we fellowship with, or a husband or wife, Jesus is the friend and partner whose presence calms the storms of our lives.

Although within the Church we should find these three things, friendship, fellowship, and partnership, if we don't find them there, we do find them in the person and work of Christ. Jesus is all these things to us. He is our fellowship, our friend, and great partner who is the lover of our souls.

Many people when they are lonely, instead of turning to Christ, turn to poor substitutes to fill the empty void in their lives. They may turn to drugs, sex, materialism, worldly friends, and worldly interests. But only the Lord Jesus can truly satisfy our souls and take away our loneliness. The great hymn writers knew this and so we find this in their hymns.

I Never Walk Alone

I never walk alone, I have the Savior,
Who walks beside me everywhere I go:
My heart rejoices in His loving favor,
And all who will His saving grace may know.

I never walk alone, in stormy weather,
When winds of trouble sweep about my head,
I know I'm safe, because we are together,
And round me His protecting love is spread.

I never walk alone, Christ walks beside me,
He is the dearest Friend I've ever known.
With such a Friend to comfort and to guide me,
I never, no, never walk alone.

—Alfred H. Ackley

Yes, Jesus is the friend of sinners. Jesus is the lover of our souls. Jesus is the One who walks with us and fellowships with us all through our lives here below on this side of the veil of tears. Yes, Jesus provides for the lonely. How does He do that? He gives Himself to us! This is the greatest gift and the most comforting gift we could ever have or receive. Jesus will never leave us or forsake us. He'll be with us in our times of loneliness, sorrow, grief, or pain. We remember the story of the three Hebrew youths in the fiery furnace in Babylon in Daniel's book. There was a fourth man in the fire. Jesus is the fourth man in the fire. When you are in the fires and furnaces of life, Jesus will be there for you too!

Charles Bridges suggests the following steps to be taken by those who find they are lonely. Bridges was a preacher from the Church of England. He was excellent in diagnosing the needs of those who sat under his ministry. Here are the steps he suggests to overcome loneliness:

1. Cultivate a personal relationship with Christ.
2. Set a high value on Christ's friendship.
3. Make Christ the constant subject of your thoughts and conversation.
4. Avoid whatever is displeasing to Christ.
5. Follow Christ in your youth, and delight in Him in your old age. [2]

12
The Peace Of God

Isaiah. 26:3, "You will keep him in perfect peace, Whose mind is stayed on You, Because he trusts in You."

This is one of those verses that will always be a favorite among God's people. It is because of the nature of life and our existence upon earth. Our lives are often filled with tragedies, difficulties, sorrows, and burdens. How we need peace in such a troubled world. We must remember there is a difference between "the peace with God" and "the peace of God."

1. Peace with God—refers to our justification, the removal of our guilt and sin through the finished work of Christ.

2. Peace of God—refers to our sanctification and our growth in grace, our ability to rest in God's promises and grace.

Peace with God through redemption always comes first. But in our text I believe the prophet has the "peace of God" in mind. This is similar to Philippians 4:7, "And the peace of God, which passeth all understanding, shall keep your hearts and minds through Christ Jesus."

Before we break our text down let me give you the background and meaning of this verse. This chapter was a song of joy over Judah's consolation. This is a continuation of the song in the preceding chapter. Calvin says it was actually written before the Jews were taken into captivity into Babylon. This was to prepare His people before they faced actual suffering. This shows us how God even anticipates our problems and prepares for them. This was to help His people bear up under the trials before and while they faced them. Some expositors see in this passage a spiritual portrayal of the church. Its primary meaning refers to the Jews in Babylon being delivered. Its secondary meaning refers to all sinners being delivered from sin. The meaning of the words in this text:

- Perfect peace—a superlative that lit. means "peace, peace," "Shalom, Shalom."

- Mind—thoughts, imagination, or desires.

- Stayed—this word is rich in meaning. It means "to hang on, to have a firm hold, to be fixed upon, to rest in, to be devoted to, to stop at."

- Trusts—to take refuge in.

- Peace—serenity, calmness, happiness, which only the Spirit of God can give us.

I want us to look at the peace of God as we see it in this text in Isaiah. There will be three things that we will look at and examine:

- The Source Of This Peace
- The Strength Of This Peace
- The Scope Of This Peace

The Source Of This Peace
"You will keep…"

This peace is from the Lord. It cannot be sought apart from Him. William Hendrickson, a famous Bible expositor, says, "It is the God-given reward resulting from joyful reflection on God's bounties."[1] (blessings) The word *keep* is from the Hebrew word *natsar* and means "to guard and to preserve that which is being besieged or attacked." Sometimes we are besieged. Many times we are spiritually attacked. We need God's grace to keep us in times of trial, stress, fear and confusion. Isaiah 41:10 reads, "Fear not, for I am with you; Be not dismayed, for I am your God. I will strengthen you, Yes, I will help you, I will uphold you with My righteous right hand.'" And the apostle Paul tells us in Philippians 4:13, "I can do all things through Christ who strengthens me." What a blessing is the grace and peace of God that we partake of through the finished work of Christ. Another pastor speaks of this peace that passes all understanding in this way:

> "God's peace 'passes understanding.' It is simply unfathomable. There is a great sea of it! This peace cannot be adequately described but it can be experienced by God's praying children. 'Peace' is the soul's calm after it has been stilled by the command of the Savior." [2]

C.H. Spurgeon explains why this peace is called the peace of God. Spurgeon writes:

> "...why is this called 'the peace of God?' We suppose it is because it comes from God—because it was planned by God—because God gave His Son to make the peace—because God gives His Spirit to give the peace in the conscience—because, indeed, it is God

Himself in the soul, reconciled to man, whose is the peace. And while it is true that this man shall have the peace—even the Man-Christ, yet we know it is because He was the God-Christ that He was our peace."[3]

Many times God subdues our enemies. Proverbs 16:7, "When a man's ways please the Lord, He makes even his enemies to be at peace with him."

The Strength Of This Peace
"whose mind is stayed on You."

This peace comes from a continual reflection and meditation upon Christ and trust in His promises. The following verses make this very clear for us:

- John 6:37, "All that the Father gives Me will come to Me, and the one who comes to Me I will by no means cast out."

- Matthew 11:28-30, "Come to Me, all you who labor and are heavy laden, and I will give you rest. Take My yoke upon you and learn from Me, for I am gentle and lowly in heart, and you will find rest for your souls. For My yoke is easy and My burden is light."

- Mathew 28:19-20, "Go therefore and make disciples of all the nations, baptizing them in the name of the Father and of the Son and of the Holy Spirit, teaching them to observe all things that I have commanded you; and lo, I am with you always, even to the end of the age." Amen."

- John 15:5, "I am the vine, you are the branches. He who abides in Me, and I in him, bears much fruit; for without Me you can do nothing."

A good translation of Isaiah 26:3, could be, "Thou wilt keep him in absolute peace, whose imagination stops at thee because he takes refuge in thee." How we torment ourselves with unnecessary problems, trying to look ahead and figure out the possible difficulties, snares, or fears we may have to face. We should refuse to allow our minds to torment us so. Jesus gives us great counsel in Matthew. 6:25-34:

> "Therefore I say to you, do not worry about your life, what you will eat or what you will drink; nor about your body, what you will put on. Is not life more than food and the body more than clothing? Look at the birds of the air, for they neither sow nor reap nor gather into barns; yet your heavenly Father feeds them. Are you not of more value than they? Which of you by worrying can add one cubit

The Scope Of This Peace
It Is "Perfect Peace"

By scope we mean its extent, its magnitude. The Hebrew for *peace* in this text is literally—"peace, peace." This peace that we find from gazing upon our God is a superlative peace, an abundant and overflowing peace. This peace that God gives is real as opposed to that which is false or spurious. This perfect peace does not mean we will never face problems, discouragements or difficulties, but it does mean that in the midst of our sorrows, our hearts can find peace and rest. A good example of this is when the children of Israel found themselves in captivity in Babylon. The people of Babylon demanded of the Jews to sing some of their songs of Zion. They wanted to hear the praises of the people of God. But the people were too deeply grieved to be able to sing. They cried out, "How shall we sing the Lord's song in a strange land?" Psalm 137:4. But O how wrong these weary captives were. The sweet praises of Israel are always sung best when in a strange land. The darker our trials the sweeter is His presence among us. We must all learn that no matter how dark the night or how trying the situation, if we keep our eyes and our gaze fixed on Christ, He will keep us in perfect peace. The Bible is full of these kinds of examples. The Jews failed to see that the Lord's song can be sung anywhere and at anytime! Moses on the mountain was on holy ground. Jacob in the wilderness had his Bethel.

The Lord's song is always sung best in a strange land. (By strange I mean in times of stress and trial). Consider how the following men were able to praise God in the most difficult circumstances:

- Jacob in the wilderness.
- David in exile.
- John Bunyan in Bedford jail.
- John Milton in his blindness.
- Samuel Rutherford in his banishment.
- Jesus, the night He was betrayed.
- Paul and Silas in prison.

What an overwhelming promise this verse is in Isaiah! What a wonderful God we have! What a refuge in times of spiritual storm! But the implication of this text is that we must take delight in God; in His being, in His character, and in His promises. We must cultivate His companionship and His friendship. With too many of us, God is only a theological definition or proposition to be discussed or debated. He is not One with whom we walk or daily delight ourselves in. We must change this in order to enjoy the peace of God.

When we are tried and tested, we need to survey the wondrous cross of our Lord and Savior Jesus Christ.

When I Survey The Wondrous Cross

When I survey the wondrous cross
On which the Prince of glory died,
My richest gains I count but loss,
And pour contempt on all my pride.

Forbid it Lord, that I should boast,
Save in the death of Christ my God.
All the vain things that charm me most,
I sacrifice them to his blood.

See from His head, His feet, His side,
Sorrow and love flow mingled down?
Did ere such love or sorrow meet,
Or thorns compose so rich a crown?

His dying crimson like a robe,
Spreads ore' His body on the tree,
And I am dead to all the world,
And all the world is dead to me.

Where the whole realm of nature mine,
That were a present far to small.
Love so amazing so divine,
Demands my life, my soul, my all.

—Isaac Watts

Conclusion

We have been looking at this subject of finding peace in times of pain. Life has it's overwhelming share of moments of pain. Life is filled with disappointments, periods of spiritual darkness, and times of total and utter despair. We should not be surprised at this, for we read in the Bible that this is a fallen world. I am not surprised that we have so many of these discouraging moments. I am surprised that they are not more frequent than they are. When I study the Bible's teaching on the total depravity of man, I cannot for the life of me understand why the Lord does not send us all to hell. Even in the hard providences of life I am surprised that the Lord overrules on our behalf as much as He does. What grace and blessing is ours that our kind and sovereign heavenly Father is so patient and restrained with us in our daily sorrows.

"He will not always strive with us, nor will He keep His anger forever. He has not dealt with us according to our sins, nor punished us according to our iniquities. For as the heavens are high above the earth, so great is His mercy toward those who fear Him. As far as the east is from the west, so far has He removed our transgressions from us. As a father pities his children, so the Lord pities those who fear Him. For He knows our frame; He remembers that we are dust." Psalm 103:8-14.

This Thing Is From Me

However, we also need to remind ourselves that whatever happens in our lives as Christians is divinely appointed by our Father in Heaven, who is too wise to err and to loving to be unkind. In I Kings 12:24 we read where the Lord spoke to a prophet named Shemiah to give a message to the King of Judah. The Israelites were rebelling against the Kingdom of Judah and the King of Judah raised a great army and went out to fight against the rebels. But the Word of the Lord came to the prophet Shemiah and told him to not go up to fight the children of Israel. The Lord told the King, "You shall not go up nor fight against your brethren the children of Israel. Let every man return to his house for this thing is from Me." What an amazing statement, "…this thing is from Me." May we all hear this carefully. The trials and temptations of life are providences that are sent from the Lord. Nothing happens but that it is a part of the revealed and permissive will of the Lord. The apostle Paul tells us in Romans 8:28, "And we know that all things work together for good to those who love God, to those who are the called according to His purpose." Do we really grasp this message? Everything that happens in our lives is sent from the Lord. "This thing is from Me." This is the message the Lord wants us to know. In Job 23:10 we read, "But He knows the way that I take; when He has tested me, I shall come forth as gold." Every trial, every test, every moment of pain, is from the throne of God. Every disappointment, every sorrow, and every tear is ordained by the hand of our Father in heaven. When He puts us through the furnace, we will come out of these moments as gold refined by the same fire that we so much dreaded. Dear child of God, understand this great truth. The Lord brings things into your life, and although you may suffer immeasurably from them, they are designed to mold and shape you into the image of Christ. Suffering and sorrows are part of the divine school the Lord has enrolled each of us in to put us through the fire so that we will be like a diamond that has been polished and buffed by the hammer and chisel. When God has finished with us in this divine school, we will be vessels capable of reflecting the glory of God in ways we never could have imagined.

We must not forget the Lord is the sovereign ruler over every event of our lives. Whatever we face on a daily basis, it is something sent to us from the hand of our Creator and Lord. Do you not know that He is more concerned for your well being than you are for yourself? God is not taken by surprise by your sorrows or your suffering. He has planned it all. He, who brought you to it, will bring you through it. Our God, who is manifested in three persons of the Father, the Son, and the Holy Spirit is more concerned for you than you could ever be for yourself. The Lord would remind us that "...he who touches you touches the apple of His eye." Zechariah 2:8. The God who chose us, who sent His Son to live and die for us, whose Spirit has drawn us to Christ and created in our hearts a hunger for God, this great and mighty God has set His eternal and electing love upon you. You are special to Him in ways we can never fathom this side of eternity. Our God has actually taken up residence in our hearts and made us His Holy Place. Every child of God, no matter how humble or how insignificant they feel, are the temple and dwelling place of the eternal God. Who can fathom such a thought? We have the privilege to know God, to fellowship with God, to worship God, to walk with God, and to be the friend of God. This knowledge is almost too wonderful to comprehend.

When you are tempted, remember "this thing is from Me." When you are buffeted by bashing storms of life, and tossed to and fro on the wild tides of the raging seas of providence, remember that "this thing is from Me." When you are sick, weary, lonely, feel deserted and worthless, remember "this thing is from Me." Never forget, as the Psalmist has said, "Weeping may endure for a night but joy cometh in the morning." Psalm 30:5. If we would be used and blessed by the Lord, we must be willing to be broken in the hands of God as Jesus broke the bread in His hands that fed the multitudes. If we would desire to be a blessing to others, we must be willing to be broken and spilled out as was the costly ointment that was poured out of the broken vessel and poured onto our Savior by the worshipping woman. Never forget the Word of the Lord tells us that, "…my God shall supply all your need according to His riches in glory by Christ Jesus." Philippians 4:19.

What have we learned from our journey through this book? We learned in John 16:33 that in the world we shall have tribulation. But the good news is that Jesus has overcome the world and will be there with us in these times of sorrow and suffering to help us overcome as well. We learned in Hebrews 10:32-36 the proper way to handle the sufferings of life. We learned we should respond with praise, thanksgiving, and profound joy. Amazing! We learned from Romans 8:28 that all things (good or bad) work together for good to all those who love the Lord. From Samson's riddle we learned that from the devouring and bitter experiences of life come our sweetest lessons. We learned from Hebrews 2:3 that no one is too great a sinner that they cannot be saved. What hope is held out from the finished work of the Son of God! We learned once again from Romans 8:28 of the overwhelming peace that comes to those who love God. We learned in Psalm 137 that we are indeed able to sing and praise the Lord in a strange land. In Isaiah 40:1 we discovered the sweet comfort that God pours on all those who are passing through the fires of suffering and sorrow. From Psalm 42:1-11 we saw how God comforts those who are overwhelmed with discouragement. We learned in Proverbs 18:28 that Jesus is closer than a brother and that He is able to comfort all those who are lonely and desolate. Finally, in Isaiah 26:3, we discovered the peace of God that is poured out upon all those who keep their minds focused on God and on His Son Jesus Christ. God has a purpose for all the trials and sufferings we pass through in life. Someone wisely said it is from the hands of those who have suffered that comes the kindness, graciousness, mercy, and healing the world so desperately needs.

> "Lighthouses are built by shipwrecked sailors. Roads are widened by mangled motorists. Hospitals are built by those who were sick. Compassionate counselors come from those who have been broken. Good listeners come from those who have been lonely. True friends come from those who

were once deserted. Great understanding comes from those who have experienced trials the most. Where nobody suffers, nobody cares. When you suffer you learn to care. That is why God does not comfort us to make us comfortable, but to make us comforters."

If we have suffered greatly, if we have sorrowed deeply, or if we have grieved more acutely, it is very likely that the Lord has been preparing us to be a blessing to multitudes of wounded suffering believers that will providentially come into our lives.

I want to leave you with this great statement from the apostle Paul as he tells us about the comfort that comes from the Lord of all the universe:

> "Blessed be the God and Father of our Lord Jesus Christ, the Father of mercies and God of all comfort; who comforts us in all our affliction so that we may be able to comfort those who are in any affliction with the comfort with which we ourselves are comforted by God. For just as the sufferings of Christ are ours in abundance, so also our comfort is abundant through Christ." II Corinthians 1:3-5

Endnotes

Chapter One

1. Peter Jeffery, quoting J. C. Ryle in *Sickness and Death—in the Christian Family*, (Evangelical Press, 1993), p. 15.
2. Elizabeth Elliot, *On Asking Why*, (Fleming H. Revell Company, New Jersey, 1989), p. 16-17.
3. Elizabeth Elliot, Ibid. p. 21-22.

Chapter Two

1. William R. Newell, *Hebrews Verse By Verse*, (Moody Press, 1978), p. 363.
2. Gordon J. Keddie, *The Practical Christian, James Simply Explained*, (Evangelical Press, 1989), p. 24.
3. C. H. Spurgeon, *The Treasury of David Vol. III*, (Zondervan Publishing House, 1974), p. 271-272.

Chapter Three

1. J.C. Brumfield, *Comfort For Troubled Christians*. (Moody Publishers, 1961), p. 43.
2. R.C. Sproul, *Loving God*, From the Internet, Goodreads.com

Chapter Four

1. David Dickson, Quoted *In Peace And Truth*, 2012:1.
2. Thomas Brooks, from the internet: https://sites.google.com/site/evangelictheology/p/p0000004/pl00002/psalm119teth65to72
3. Martin Luther, Ibid.
4. J.C. Brumfield, *Comfort For Troubled Christians*, (Moody Publishers, 1961), p. 52.

Chapter Five

1. Thomas Walsh, *The great salvation; and the danger of neglecting it.* A sermon on Hebrews ii. 3. 1730-1759.
2. Dr. Martyn Lloyd-Jones, "What Makes Salvation So Great," December 18, 2017. Adapted from *Studies in the Book of Hebrews.*

Chapter Six

1. Sharon James, Evangelical Press.
2. E. Stanley Jones, Quoted by Gordon MaDonald, *A Resilient Life*, (Thomas Nelson Publishers, 2004).
3. George Matheson, *Thoughts For Life's Journey.*
4. John Newton, In a letter to a friend.

Chapter Seven

1. Andrew Bonar.
2. C.S. Lewis, *Reflections*, p. 113.
3. C.H. Spurgeon, *The Treasury of David*, Vol. 3b, p. 226.
4. James Montgomery Boice, *Expository Commentary*.

Chapter Eight

1. John Owen, from the internet, http://christian-quotes.ochristian.com/Comfort-Quotes/page-3.shtml
2. Alexander Whyte, Ibid.
3. C.H. Spurgeon From The Sermon, *Comfort Ye My People, Isaiah 40*:1.

Chapter Nine

1. Got Questions, From the Internet: https://www.gotquestions.org/overcoming-discouragement.html

Chapter Ten

1. David Brainard, quoted by C.H. Spurgeon, A Sermon, (No. 43) Delivered on Sabbath Morning, September 9, 1855, by the New Park Street Chapel, Southwark.

Chapter Eleven

1. Got Questions, from the internet: https://www.gotquestions.org/loneliness.html
2. Charles Bridges.

Chapter Twelve

1. William Hendrickson, *New Testament Commentary: Philippians*, (Grand Rapids).
2. Zack Meadows Guess, *Commentary on Paul's Letter to the Philippians*, 2017, p. 114.
3. C.H. Spurgeon, "How to Keep the Heart," February 21, 1858, *Philippians 4:7, New Park Street Pulpit Volume 4*.

www.ingramcontent.com/pod-product-compliance
Lightning Source LLC
Chambersburg PA
CBHW032114090426
42743CB00007B/349